GOODSON MUMBA

HUMANOMICS

Integrating Humanity into Economic Theory and Practice

Copyright © 2024 by Goodson Mumba

All rights reserved. No part of this publication may be reproduced, stored or transmitted in any form or by any means, electronic, mechanical, photocopying, recording, scanning, or otherwise without written permission from the publisher. It is illegal to copy this book, post it to a website, or distribute it by any other means without permission.

First edition

ISBN: 9798333953322

This book was professionally typeset on Reedsy. Find out more at reedsy.com

Contents

Preface		v
Acknowledgement		viii
Dedication		ix
Disclaimer		x
1	Chapter One: The Human Behavior in Economic Systems	1
2	Chapter Two: Human-Centered Economic Models	15
3	Chapter Three: Human Capital and Development	28
4	Chapter Four: Inequality and Social Justice	42
5	Chapter Five: Human-Centered Business Practices	55
6	Chapter Six: Globalization's Impact on Human Welfare:...	69
7	Chapter Seven: The Future Trends of Work and Automation	84
8	Chapter Eight: Behavioral Insights for Policy Making	98
9	Chapter Nine: Community Development and Empowerment	113
10	Chapter Ten: Human-Centered Financial Systems	127
11	Chapter eleven: Psychology of Economic Policy	141

12	Chapter Twelve: Cultural Economics and Creative Industries	156
13	Chapter Thirteen: Happiness Economics and Well-Being	172
14	Chapter Fourteen: Social Networks and Economic Behavior	186
15	Chapter Fifteen: Human Rights and Economic Development	200
About the Author		218

Preface

In the realm of economics, where numbers and equations often reign supreme, there exists a profound paradox—one that speaks to the inherent complexity and humanity that underpins every economic decision, transaction, and system. It is within this paradox that the seeds of "Humanomics: Integrating Humanity into Economic Theory and Practice" were sown.

This book is not just another addition to the vast literature on economics. It is a bold exploration—an invitation to journey beyond the confines of traditional economic thinking and embrace a more holistic and humane approach to understanding and shaping our economic systems.

In the pages that follow, you will encounter a diverse tapestry of ideas, perspectives, and narratives—all woven together with a common thread: the recognition of humanity as the beating heart of economics. From the bustling streets of Metropolis to the boardrooms of multinational corporations, from the corridors of power to the grassroots movements for social justice, "Humanomics" takes you on a transformative voyage—one that challenges preconceived notions, sparks new insights, and inspires action.

Through the lens of human behavior, emotions, social interactions, and cultural influences, we delve into the intricacies of economic systems, uncovering the profound ways in which human values, aspirations, and experiences shape the world of commerce and finance.

We explore the power of empathy, cooperation, and solidarity in building resilient economies that prioritize the well-being of all individuals, regardless of their background or circumstances. We confront the stark realities of inequality, injustice, and environmental degradation, while also illuminating pathways towards a more equitable, sustainable, and inclusive future.

Drawing upon the latest research, real-world examples, and timeless wisdom, "Humanomics" offers a roadmap for reimagining economics as a force for good—a tool for fostering human flourishing, promoting social progress, and safeguarding the planet we call home.

But "Humanomics" is not just a theoretical treatise—it is a call to action. It challenges economists, policymakers, business leaders, activists, and citizens alike to embrace their role as stewards of humanity and architects of a better world. It invites us to transcend the narrow confines of self-interest and short-term gain, and to embrace a vision of economics that is grounded in compassion, justice, and solidarity.

As you embark on this intellectual odyssey, I urge you to approach each chapter with an open mind and a courageous heart. Allow yourself to be challenged, inspired, and empowered to join the ranks of those who dare to dream of a more humane and just economic order.

For in the end, the true measure of "Humanomics" lies not in the words on these pages, but in the actions they inspire and the lives they touch. May this book serve as a beacon of hope, guiding us towards a future where economics truly serves humanity—a future where every individual can thrive, and where the dignity and worth of every human being are upheld and celebrated.

Welcome to "Humanomics: Integrating Humanity into Economic Theory and Practice." The journey begins now.

Sincerely,

Goodson Mumba

Acknowledgement

I would like to eternally and gratefully acknowledge the Almighty God for the infinite intelligence from His universal mind where we draw from all that we come to know and are yet to know. May I also acknowledge and thank everyone that has played a part in my journey of life in terms of spiritual, moral, emotional and material support.

Dedication

I extend my sincerest gratitude to my beloved wife, Edith Mumba, and our children, Angelina, Lubuto, Letticia, Lulumbi, and Butusho, for their unwavering support and understanding throughout the conception, writing, and eventual publication of this book, despite the sacrifices and challenges they endured.

Disclaimer

This book is a work of fiction. Names, characters, businesses, places, events, and incidents are either the products of the author's imagination or used in a fictitious manner. Any resemblance to actual persons, living or dead, or actual events is purely coincidental.

1

Chapter One: The Human Behavior in Economic Systems

The city of Lusaka buzzed with energy, its streets crowded with people rushing to and fro, each driven by their own motivations. Among them was Dr. Olivia, a renowned economist with a furrowed brow and a mind filled with questions.

As she made her way through the throngs of people, Dr. Olivia couldn't shake the feeling of disillusionment that had settled over her like a heavy fog. For years, she had dedicated herself to the study of economics, only to find herself increasingly at odds with the cold calculations and impersonal algorithms that dominated the field.

Entering her office at the prestigious Lusaka Chamber of Commerce, Dr. Olivia sighed heavily as she glanced at the towering stacks of papers littering her desk. Reports, charts, and graphs—all meticulously crafted to quantify the ineffable complexities of human behavior.

But as she reached for her coffee mug, her gaze fell upon a slender volume nestled among the clutter—a book with a simple title: "Humanomics: Integrating Humanity into Economic Theory and Practice."

Intrigued, Dr. Olivia picked up the book and began to read, her eyes widening with each page turned. Here, in these words, was a radical departure from everything she had ever known about economics. No longer were people reduced to mere cogs in a vast machine of production and consumption. Instead, they were depicted as complex beings driven by emotions, desires, and aspirations.

The more Dr. Olivia read, the more she felt a glimmer of hope flicker to life within her. Perhaps, just perhaps, there was a way to reconcile the cold logic of economics with the warm embrace of humanity.

Meanwhile, across town, Marcus paced back and forth in his sleek corporate office, his brow furrowed with worry. As the CEO of Johnson Enterprises, he had built his empire on the relentless pursuit of profit, but lately, he couldn't shake the feeling that something was missing.

Turning to his bookshelf, Marcus's gaze fell upon a familiar title—"Humanomics: Integrating Humanity into Economic Theory and Practice." He had picked up the book on a whim, never expecting it to hold any real answers to his existential crisis.

But as he flipped through its pages, Marcus felt a sense of clarity wash over him like a cool breeze on a hot summer's day. Here, in these words, was a vision of economics that transcended mere profit and loss—a vision that placed human values at its very core.

Meanwhile, in the bustling streets of Lusaka's marginalized neighborhoods, Sofia fought tirelessly against the tide of economic inequality that threatened to engulf her community.

CHAPTER ONE: THE HUMAN BEHAVIOR IN ECONOMIC SYSTEMS

Armed with little more than her passion and determination, she had dedicated herself to the cause of social justice, but lately, it felt like an uphill battle with no end in sight.

One day, as she leafed through a stack of dusty books in the local library, Sofia's fingers brushed against the spine of a slender volume—"Humanomics: Integrating Humanity into Economic Theory and Practice." Intrigued, she began to read, her eyes widening with each page turned.

Here, in these words, was a new way of thinking about economics—a way that prioritized the well-being of people over the pursuit of profit. Inspired by what she read, Sofia set out to spread the message of humanomics far and wide, determined to create a more equitable society for all.

And so, as the sun set over the city of Lusaka, Dr. Olivia, Marcus, Sofia, and countless others found themselves drawn together by the promise of a brighter future—a future where humanity and economics were no longer at odds, but inextricably intertwined in a harmonious dance of progress and prosperity.

Understanding Human Behavior in Economic Systems

As the evening descended upon the city of Lusaka, Dr. Olivia found herself immersed in the pages of "Humanomics: Integrating Humanity into Economic Theory and Practice." With each word, she felt as though a veil was being lifted from her eyes, revealing a world of possibilities she had never dared to imagine.

One particular subpoint caught her attention: "Understanding Human Behavior in Economic Systems." It spoke to the very heart of her disillusionment with traditional economics—

the notion that people were rational actors driven solely by self-interest.

But as Dr. Olivia delved deeper into the text, she encountered a different perspective—one that acknowledged the complexities of human psychology and the myriad factors that influenced economic decision-making.

Lost in thought, Dr. Olivia's mind wandered back to her own experiences as an economist, grappling with the disconnect between economic theory and the messy reality of human behavior.

Meanwhile, across town, Marcus found himself equally engrossed in the pages of "Humanomics." The subpoint on understanding human behavior resonated deeply with him, stirring memories of countless boardroom meetings and corporate negotiations.

For years, Marcus had operated under the assumption that people were rational actors motivated solely by profit. But as he read on, he began to see the flaws in this simplistic view—a view that had led him to sacrifice his own values in pursuit of financial success.

With a newfound sense of clarity, Marcus vowed to approach his business endeavors with a deeper understanding of human behavior, recognizing the importance of empathy and compassion in every transaction.

Meanwhile, Sofia continued her crusade for social justice, armed with the insights gleaned from "Humanomics." The subpoint on understanding human behavior served as a powerful reminder of the struggles faced by marginalized communities—their hopes, their fears, their dreams.

With renewed determination, Sofia set out to amplify the voices of those who had been silenced by economic inequality, using her newfound understanding of human behavior to advocate for change at every turn.

And so, as the night stretched on and the city of Lusaka slept, Dr. Olivia, Marcus, Sofia, and countless others found themselves united by a common purpose—to challenge the assumptions of traditional economics and pave the way for a more humane approach to economic theory and practice.

Emotions and Decision Making in Economic Transactions

As the city of Lusaka settled into the quiet embrace of night, Dr. Olivia found herself captivated by the subpoint within "Humanomics" titled "Emotions and Decision Making in Economic Transactions." The words leaped off the page, resonating deeply with her own experiences as an economist navigating the turbulent waters of human behavior.

In the dim glow of her desk lamp, Dr. Olivia pondered the implications of this revelation. For too long, economics had treated emotions as mere noise in the pursuit of rational decision-making. But as she read on, she realized that emotions were not distractions to be ignored, but powerful drivers that shaped every economic transaction.

Memories flooded Dr. Olivia's mind—memories of clients driven by fear, greed, love, and hope. Each emotion, she realized, played a pivotal role in shaping their economic choices, often in ways that defied traditional economic logic.

Across town, Marcus found himself similarly transfixed by the subpoint on emotions and decision-making. As he sat alone in his office, bathed in the soft glow of lamplight, he couldn't help but reflect on his own experiences as an entrepreneur.

The memories came flooding back—the exhilaration of closing a lucrative deal, the crushing weight of failure, the joy of seeing his employees thrive. Emotions, Marcus realized, were the invisible threads that bound him to his business and to the people he served.

With a newfound appreciation for the role of emotions in economic transactions, Marcus vowed to approach his business dealings with greater empathy and understanding, recognizing that behind every transaction lay a human story waiting to be heard.

Meanwhile, Sofia found herself grappling with the subpoint on emotions and decision-making in her own activism work. As she sat hunched over her desk, surrounded by stacks of pamphlets and protest signs, she couldn't help but wonder how emotions shaped the choices of those she sought to empower.

In the harsh light of her desk lamp, Sofia's thoughts turned to the faces she had encountered in her community—the fear in their eyes, the anger in their voices, the hope that burned bright even in the darkest of times. Emotions, she realized, were the driving force behind their fight for justice, fueling their resolve in the face of adversity.

Armed with this newfound understanding, Sofia resolved to harness the power of emotions in her activism, using empathy and compassion to forge connections with those she sought to uplift.

And so, as the night wore on and the city of Lusaka slept, Dr. Olivia, Marcus, Sofia, and countless others found themselves united by a common realization—that emotions were not obstacles to be overcome, but essential components of the human experience, shaping every economic transaction in ways both profound and complex.

Social Interactions and Economic Networks

As the city of Lusaka settled into the stillness of the night, Dr. Olivia found herself engrossed in the subpoint within "Humanomics" titled "Social Interactions and Economic Networks." The words danced across the page, igniting a spark of curiosity within her as she pondered the intricate web of relationships that underpinned economic transactions.

In the quiet solitude of her office, Dr. Olivia reflected on her own experiences studying the dynamics of economic networks. She remembered the countless hours spent poring over data, analyzing the flow of capital and goods through the city's bustling markets.

But as she read on, she realized that traditional economic theory had overlooked a crucial aspect of these networks—the human element. Behind every transaction lay a complex tapestry of social interactions, shaped by trust, reciprocity, and social norms.

Memories flooded Dr. Olivia's mind—memories of the vibrant communities that thrived within Lusaka's diverse neighborhoods. From the bustling street markets of Lusaka town to the cozy cafes of the arts district, she had witnessed firsthand the power of social networks to shape economic outcomes.

Across town, Marcus found himself equally captivated by the subpoint on social interactions and economic networks. As he leaned back in his leather chair, his gaze fixed on the city skyline glittering in the distance, he couldn't help but marvel at the interconnectedness of it all.

For years, Marcus had operated under the assumption that success was a solitary pursuit—that the key to prosperity lay in fierce competition and unwavering determination. But as he read on, he realized that the true power lay in collaboration and community.

With a newfound appreciation for the role of social networks in economic transactions, Marcus vowed to cultivate deeper connections within his own business circles, recognizing that behind every transaction lay an opportunity to build trust and goodwill.

Meanwhile, Sofia found herself grappling with the subpoint on social interactions and economic networks in her own activism work. As she sat surrounded by stacks of flyers and posters, her thoughts turned to the communities she sought to empower.

In the flickering light of her desk lamp, Sofia's mind raced with possibilities—possibilities for building solidarity, for fostering cooperation, for amplifying the voices of those who had been marginalized by society. She realized that true change could only come from working together, forging alliances across social boundaries to create a more just and equitable world.

And so, as the night wore on and the city of Lusaka slept, Dr. Olivia, Marcus, Sofia, and countless others found themselves united by a common vision—that behind every economic transaction lay a network of human connections, waiting to be nurtured and strengthened for the benefit of all.

Cultural Influences on Economic Activities

In the depths of the night, as the city of Lusaka slumbered, Dr. Olivia found herself enthralled by the subpoint within "Humanomics" titled "Cultural Influences on Economic Activities." The words danced before her eyes, painting a vivid picture of the ways in which cultural norms and values shaped the economic landscape.

Lost in thought, Dr. Olivia's mind drifted back to her own upbringing—a tapestry woven from the threads of her Chinese heritage and Western education. She remembered the lessons imparted by her parents, the traditions passed down through generations, and the values that guided her every decision.

But as she read on, she realized that her own cultural background was just one piece of the puzzle. Lusaka was a melting pot of cultures, each contributing its own unique flavor to the city's economic tapestry.

Across town, Marcus found himself equally captivated by the subpoint on cultural influences. As he sat in his office, surrounded by the trappings of success, he couldn't help but reflect on the role that culture had played in shaping his own entrepreneurial journey.

From the hustle and bustle of his immigrant parents' corner store to the sleek corporate offices of Johnson Enterprises, Marcus had navigated a world shaped by cultural norms and expectations. But as he read on, he realized that his own experiences were just one thread in the rich tapestry of Lusaka's cultural landscape.

With a newfound appreciation for the diversity of cultural influences, Marcus vowed to embrace the richness of Lusaka's cultural mosaic, recognizing that true innovation came from drawing upon a multiplicity of perspectives and experiences.

Meanwhile, Sofia found herself grappling with the subpoint on cultural influences in her activism work. As she sat in her makeshift office, surrounded by posters and flyers, she couldn't help but reflect on the ways in which cultural norms had shaped the struggles of marginalized communities.

In the dim light of her desk lamp, Sofia's thoughts turned to the immigrant neighborhoods that dotted the city—a patchwork of cultures, languages, and traditions woven together by the shared experience of displacement and struggle. She realized that in order to truly advocate for change, she needed to understand and respect the cultural nuances that shaped the lives of those she sought to empower.

And so, as the night stretched on and the city of Lusaka slept, Dr. Olivia, Marcus, Sofia, and countless others found themselves united by a common realization—that behind every economic activity lay a tapestry of cultural influences, waiting to be explored and celebrated for the richness it brought to their shared journey of discovery.

Psychology of Consumption and Saving

In the quiet of the night, with the city of Lusaka wrapped in slumber, Dr. Olivia found herself absorbed by the subpoint within "Humanomics" titled "Psychology of Consumption and Saving." The words on the page seemed to dance before her, illuminating the intricate dance between human psychology and economic behavior.

Lost in thought, Dr. Olivia's mind wandered to the countless individuals she had encountered over the years—consumers driven by desires both rational and irrational, savers hoarding

CHAPTER ONE: THE HUMAN BEHAVIOR IN ECONOMIC SYSTEMS

their resources for an uncertain future. Each decision, she realized, was influenced by a complex interplay of psychological factors.

Memories flooded Dr. Olivia's mind—memories of clients grappling with the temptation of instant gratification, the fear of financial insecurity, the euphoria of a well-earned reward. She realized that behind every purchase, every dollar saved, lay a story waiting to be told—a story of hopes, fears, and aspirations.

Across town, Marcus found himself equally captivated by the subpoint on the psychology of consumption and saving. As he sat alone in his office, surrounded by the trappings of wealth, he couldn't help but reflect on his own relationship with money.

From his early days scrimping and saving to build his first business, to the lavish spending that had become synonymous with his success, Marcus had grappled with the psychological tug-of-war between consumption and saving. But as he read on, he realized that his own struggles were just one piece of the puzzle—a puzzle shaped by the hopes and dreams of countless individuals striving for financial security and fulfillment.

With a newfound understanding of the psychology of consumption and saving, Marcus vowed to approach his own financial decisions with greater mindfulness and intentionality, recognizing that true wealth lay not in material possessions, but in the peace of mind that came from living within one's means.

Meanwhile, Sofia found herself grappling with the subpoint on the psychology of consumption and saving in her activism work. As she sat hunched over her desk, surrounded by stacks of pamphlets and posters, she couldn't help but reflect on the ways in which economic insecurity had shaped the lives of those she sought to empower.

In the soft glow of her desk lamp, Sofia's thoughts turned to the families struggling to make ends meet, the workers trapped in cycles of debt and poverty, the dreams deferred by the relentless pressures of consumer culture. She realized that in order to truly advocate for change, she needed to understand and address the psychological barriers that prevented individuals from achieving financial security and well-being.

And so, as the night wore on and the city of Lusaka slept, Dr. Olivia, Marcus, Sofia, and countless others found themselves united by a common realization—that behind every economic decision lay a complex tapestry of psychological factors, waiting to be explored and understood for the betterment of all.

Ethics and Morality in Economic Decision Making

In the stillness of the night, with the city of Lusaka wrapped in silence, Dr. Olivia found herself drawn into the subpoint within "Humanomics" titled "Ethics and Morality in Economic Decision Making." The words on the page shimmered with significance, illuminating the moral complexities that lay at the heart of economic behavior.

Lost in contemplation, Dr. Olivia's thoughts drifted to the ethical dilemmas she had encountered throughout her career—the trade-offs between profit and principle, the compromises made in the pursuit of success. Each decision, she realized, carried with it a weighty moral burden, challenging her deeply held beliefs about right and wrong.

Memories flooded Dr. Olivia's mind—memories of clients

wrestling with the moral implications of their actions, the ethical quandaries that kept them awake at night, the choices that defined their character and integrity. She realized that behind every economic decision, every balance sheet, every bottom line, lay a choice—a choice to do what was easy or what was right.

Across town, Marcus found himself equally captivated by the subpoint on ethics and morality in economic decision making. As he sat alone in his office, surrounded by the trappings of success, he couldn't help but reflect on the moral compromises he had made in the pursuit of profit.

From cutting corners to boost quarterly earnings, to turning a blind eye to the human cost of his business ventures, Marcus had grappled with the ethical implications of his actions. But as he read on, he realized that his own struggles were just one thread in the fabric of Lusaka's ethical landscape—a landscape shaped by the choices of countless individuals striving to reconcile their ambitions with their conscience.

With a newfound awareness of the ethical dimensions of economic decision making, Marcus vowed to conduct his business affairs with greater integrity and accountability, recognizing that true success could only be achieved through a commitment to ethical conduct and moral responsibility.

Meanwhile, Sofia found herself grappling with the subpoint on ethics and morality in her activism work. As she sat hunched over her desk, surrounded by stacks of petitions and protest signs, she couldn't help but reflect on the moral imperative that drove her fight for social justice.

In the soft glow of her desk lamp, Sofia's thoughts turned to the principles that guided her every action—the belief in the inherent dignity and worth of every individual, the conviction that justice could only be achieved through righteousness and compassion. She realized that in order to truly advocate for change, she needed to hold herself and others accountable to the highest ethical standards, even in the face of adversity.

And so, as the night wore on and the city of Lusaka slept, Dr. Olivia, Marcus, Sofia, and countless others found themselves united by a common realization—that behind every economic decision lay a moral choice, waiting to be made for the betterment of society and the advancement of human dignity.

2

Chapter Two: Human-Centered Economic Models

In the heart of Lusaka, amidst the towering Buildings and bustling streets, a quiet revolution was brewing. Dr. Olivia, Marcus, Sofia, and a diverse array of visionaries had come together to challenge the entrenched paradigms of traditional economics and forge a new path forward—one centered on the needs and aspirations of humanity.

As they gathered in a dimly lit conference room at the Lusaka Chamber of Commerce, anticipation hung heavy in the air. Dr. Olivia, with her piercing intellect and unwavering determination, stood at the front of the room, her eyes alight with passion as she addressed the eager audience.

"Welcome, everyone," she began, her voice ringing out with clarity and conviction. "Today, we embark on a journey to explore human-centered economic models—models that prioritize the well-being of people over the pursuit of profit."

Marcus, his youthful energy and entrepreneurial spirit shining through, stepped forward to share his own insights. "For too long, we've operated under the assumption that economic success is measured solely by financial wealth," he declared. "But true prosperity encompasses so much more—it's about fostering thriving communities, nurturing meaningful connections, and uplifting the human spirit."

Sofia, with her fierce determination and unwavering commitment to social justice, added her voice to the chorus. "In a world rife with inequality and injustice, human-centered economic models offer a beacon of hope," she proclaimed. "They empower individuals to take control of their own destinies, to forge a future that is equitable, sustainable, and just."

As the presentations continued, a sense of excitement and possibility permeated the room. Ideas flowed freely, barriers dissolved, and a shared vision of a more humane economy began to take shape.

In the days and weeks that followed, Dr. Olivia, Marcus, Sofia, and their allies worked tirelessly to bring their vision to life. They collaborated with economists, policymakers, and community leaders to develop innovative solutions that placed people at the center of economic decision-making.

From community wealth-building initiatives to cooperative business models, from universal basic income experiments to ethical investment strategies, they explored a myriad of approaches designed to empower individuals, strengthen communities, and promote shared prosperity.

And as their efforts gained momentum, the ripple effects spread far beyond the confines of Lusaka. Across the globe, people from all walks of life were inspired to embrace a new paradigm of economics—one that valued human dignity, environmental sustainability, and social justice above all else.

Critique of Traditional Economic Models

In the heart of the bustling city of Lusaka, amidst the cacophony of honking horns and bustling crowds, a group of intellectuals gathered in a dimly lit seminar room at the Lusaka Chamber of Commerce. Dr. Olivia, Marcus, Sofia, and a host of other scholars and activists had convened to dissect and critique the shortcomings of traditional economic models.

With furrowed brows and pens poised over notepads, the participants listened intently as Dr. Olivia took the floor, her voice resonating with authority and conviction.

"Our journey begins with a critical examination of the traditional economic models that have long dominated our discourse," she began, her gaze sweeping across the room. "For too long, these models have relied on simplistic assumptions and narrow frameworks that fail to capture the complexities of human behavior and societal dynamics."

Marcus, his eyes alight with passion and determination, stepped forward to share his own perspective. "Indeed," he exclaimed, his voice ringing out with conviction. "Traditional economic models often prioritize profit over people, perpetuating a cycle of inequality and exploitation that undermines the very fabric of society."

Sofia, her voice infused with a fierce sense of urgency, added her voice to the chorus. "We cannot ignore the inherent flaws of traditional economic models," she declared. "From their failure to account for externalities such as environmental degradation, to their reliance on GDP as a measure of progress, these models are ill-equipped to address the complex challenges of the modern world."

As the discussion unfolded, a sense of shared purpose and

determination permeated the room. Participants exchanged ideas, challenged assumptions, and unearthed the deep-seated flaws that had long plagued traditional economic thinking.

In the days and weeks that followed, Dr. Olivia, Marcus, Sofia, and their fellow critics embarked on a crusade to expose the shortcomings of traditional economic models to a wider audience. They published articles, gave lectures, and engaged in public debates, shining a light on the inherent contradictions and limitations of mainstream economic thought.

Their efforts did not go unnoticed. Across Lusaka and beyond, people from all walks of life began to question the status quo, demanding a more nuanced and inclusive approach to economic theory and practice.

And as the sun set over the city skyline, casting long shadows across the streets of Lusaka, Dr. Olivia, Marcus, Sofia, and their allies stood united in their commitment to forging a new path forward—a path that rejected the dogma of traditional economic models in favor of a more humane and equitable vision for the future.

Introduction to Human-Centered Economic Frameworks

In the heart of Lusaka, amidst the towering Buildings and bustling streets, a sense of anticipation hung heavy in the air as Dr. Olivia, Marcus, Sofia, and a diverse group of innovators gathered in a spacious conference hall at the Lusaka Chamber of Commerce. They had come together to introduce a new era in economic thinking—a era centered on the needs and values of humanity.

As Dr. Olivia stepped onto the stage, her presence commanded the attention of the room. With a warm smile and a twinkle in her eye, she addressed the eager audience.

"Welcome, everyone, to the dawn of a new age in economics," she began, her voice echoing through the hall. "Today, we embark on a journey to explore human-centered economic frameworks—frameworks that prioritize the well-being and dignity of every individual."

Marcus, his charisma and passion evident in every word, stepped forward to share his own insights. "For too long, economics has been driven by a narrow focus on profit and growth," he proclaimed, his voice ringing with conviction. "But true prosperity lies in nurturing thriving communities, fostering meaningful relationships, and uplifting the human spirit."

Sofia, her fiery determination and unwavering commitment to social justice shining through, added her voice to the chorus. "In a world marked by inequality and injustice, human-centered economic frameworks offer a beacon of hope," she declared. "They empower individuals to take control of their own destinies, to build a future that is equitable, sustainable, and just."

As the presentations continued, a sense of excitement and possibility filled the room. Ideas flowed freely, barriers dissolved, and a shared vision of a more humane economy began to take shape.

In the days and weeks that followed, Dr. Olivia, Marcus, Sofia, and their allies worked tirelessly to bring their vision to life. They collaborated with economists, policymakers, and community leaders to develop innovative frameworks that placed people at the center of economic decision-making.

From participatory budgeting initiatives to community-owned cooperatives, from local currency programs to impact investing strategies, they explored a myriad of approaches designed to empower individuals, strengthen communities, and promote shared prosperity.

And as their efforts gained momentum, the ripple effects spread far beyond the confines of Lusaka. Across the globe, people from all walks of life were inspired to embrace a new paradigm of economics—one that valued human dignity, environmental sustainability, and social justice above all else.

Behavioral Economics: Insights from Psychology and Sociology

In the heart of Lusaka, within the hallowed halls of the Lusaka Chamber of Commerce, a diverse group of scholars and practitioners gathered to explore the intersections of economics, psychology, and sociology. Dr. Olivia, Marcus, Sofia, and their esteemed colleagues had convened to delve into the realm of behavioral economics—a field that promised to shed new light on the complexities of human behavior and decision-making.

As they settled into their seats in a spacious lecture hall, anticipation crackled in the air. Dr. Olivia, with her keen intellect and boundless curiosity, stepped forward to address the eager audience.

"Welcome, everyone, to the frontier of economic inquiry," she began, her voice resonating with authority and enthusiasm. "Today, we embark on a journey to explore the fascinating realm of behavioral economics—a discipline that seeks to understand how psychological and sociological factors influence economic decision-making."

CHAPTER TWO: HUMAN-CENTERED ECONOMIC MODELS

Marcus, his eyes alight with excitement and intrigue, stepped forward to share his own insights. "In our quest for economic enlightenment, we must look beyond the traditional paradigms of rational choice theory," he proclaimed, his voice carrying a note of urgency. "Behavioral economics offers us a new lens through which to examine the quirks and biases that shape our decisions, revealing hidden truths about human nature and society."

Sofia, her passion for social justice burning bright, added her voice to the conversation. "By integrating insights from psychology and sociology into our economic framework, we gain a deeper understanding of the forces that drive inequality and injustice," she declared, her voice infused with determination. "We must use this knowledge to craft policies and interventions that empower individuals and communities, fostering a more equitable and compassionate society."

As the presentations continued, a sense of excitement and possibility filled the room. Participants exchanged ideas, challenged assumptions, and unearthed profound insights into the human condition.

In the days and weeks that followed, Dr. Olivia, Marcus, Sofia, and their fellow scholars embarked on a journey of discovery, exploring the myriad ways in which psychological and sociological factors influenced economic behavior. They conducted experiments, analyzed data, and collaborated with experts from across disciplines to unravel the mysteries of human decision-making.

Their efforts yielded groundbreaking insights into the irrationality of human behavior, the power of social norms, and the importance of empathy and compassion in economic transactions. Armed with this knowledge, they set out to reshape economic theory and practice, forging a new path forward that prioritized human welfare and societal well-being.

And as their work gained recognition and acclaim, the ripple effects spread far beyond the confines of Lusaka. Across the globe, policymakers, economists, and activists alike embraced the principles of behavioral economics, using them to inform policies and interventions that promoted social justice, environmental sustainability, and economic prosperity for all.

Socioeconomic Models: Integrating Social Factors into Economic Analysis

In the heart of Lusaka, where the rhythm of the city pulses through the streets, a group of scholars and thinkers gathered at the Lusaka Chamber of Commerce. Dr. Olivia, Marcus, Sofia, and a cohort of intellectuals had come together to explore the intricacies of socioeconomic models—a realm where economic analysis intersected with the dynamics of society.

As they convened in a sunlit seminar room, the air crackled with anticipation. Dr. Olivia, with her keen intellect and commanding presence, stepped forward to address the assembled audience.

"Welcome, esteemed colleagues, to the forefront of economic inquiry," she began, her voice resounding with authority. "Today, we embark on a journey to unravel the complexities of socioeconomic models—a discipline that seeks to integrate social factors into economic analysis, illuminating the intricate web of relationships that shape our world."

Marcus, his passion for innovation palpable, stepped forward to share his perspective. "In our quest for economic understanding, we must recognize the interconnectedness of economic systems and social structures," he declared, his voice brimming with enthusiasm. "Socioeconomic models offer us a holistic framework through which to examine the multifaceted nature of human society, capturing the interplay between economics, politics, culture, and beyond."

Sofia, her commitment to social justice unwavering, added her voice to the conversation. "By integrating social factors into our economic analysis, we gain a deeper appreciation for the complexities of inequality and injustice," she asserted, her voice infused with determination. "We must use this knowledge to advocate for policies and interventions that promote equity, inclusion, and empowerment for all members of society."

As the discussion unfolded, a sense of possibility filled the room. Ideas flowed freely, barriers dissolved, and a shared vision of a more just and equitable future began to take shape.

In the days and weeks that followed, Dr. Olivia, Marcus, Sofia, and their fellow scholars delved deep into the intricacies of socioeconomic models. They analyzed data, conducted research, and collaborated with experts from diverse disciplines to develop comprehensive frameworks that captured the nuances of human society.

Their efforts yielded profound insights into the root causes of inequality, the dynamics of social mobility, and the impact of policy interventions on the fabric of society. Armed with this knowledge, they set out to inform public discourse, shape policy agendas, and advocate for change at the highest levels of government and academia.

And as their work gained traction, the ripple effects spread far beyond the confines of Lusaka. Across the globe, policymakers, economists, and activists alike embraced the principles of socioeconomic modeling, using them to inform policies and interventions that promoted social cohesion, economic prosperity, and human flourishing for all.

Feminist Economics: Gender Perspectives in Economic Theory

In the heart of Lusaka, where the city's heartbeat thrummed through the streets, a gathering of scholars and advocates converged at the Lusaka Chamber of Commerce. Dr. Olivia, Marcus, Sofia, and a cohort of forward-thinkers had assembled to delve into the realm of feminist economics—a domain where economic theory intersected with gender perspectives.

As they congregated in a sunlit lecture hall, the atmosphere hummed with anticipation. Dr. Olivia, her intellect sharp and her determination unwavering, stepped forward to address the attentive audience.

"Welcome, esteemed colleagues, to the forefront of economic discourse," she began, her voice carrying the weight of authority. "Today, we embark on a journey to explore the nuanced terrain of feminist economics—a discipline that sheds light on the gendered dimensions of economic theory and practice."

Marcus, his enthusiasm palpable, stepped forward to lend his perspective. "In our pursuit of economic understanding, we must recognize the profound impact of gender on our socio-economic systems," he proclaimed, his voice brimming with conviction. "Feminist economics offers us a lens through which to examine the disparities, biases, and injustices that

CHAPTER TWO: HUMAN-CENTERED ECONOMIC MODELS

persist within our economic structures, paving the way for a more inclusive and equitable future."

Sofia, her commitment to social justice unyielding, added her voice to the conversation. "By centering gender perspectives in our economic analysis, we gain insights into the ways in which economic systems perpetuate inequality and discrimination," she asserted, her voice imbued with passion. "We must use this knowledge to advocate for policies and practices that dismantle barriers, empower marginalized communities, and foster gender equity in all aspects of life."

As the dialogue unfolded, a sense of urgency filled the room. Ideas flowed freely, perspectives expanded, and a shared vision of a more just and equitable society took root.

In the days and weeks that followed, Dr. Olivia, Marcus, Sofia, and their fellow scholars delved deep into the nuances of feminist economics. They scrutinized data, interrogated assumptions, and collaborated with experts from diverse backgrounds to challenge the status quo and envision a more inclusive future.

Their efforts yielded profound insights into the intersectionality of gender, race, class, and other axes of identity. Armed with this knowledge, they set out to advocate for policies and interventions that addressed the root causes of gender inequality, empowered marginalized communities, and promoted social justice for all.

And as their work gained momentum, the ripple effects spread far beyond the confines of Lusaka. Across the globe, policymakers, economists, and activists alike embraced the principles of feminist economics, using them to inform policies and practices that transformed lives, dismantled barriers, and built a more equitable world for generations to come.

Ecological Economics: Balancing Human Needs with Environmental Sustainability

In the heart of Lusaka, where the city's skyline stretched towards the heavens, a gathering of scholars and environmentalists converged at the Lusaka Chamber of Commerce. Dr. Olivia, Marcus, Sofia, and a coalition of advocates had gathered to explore the realm of ecological economics—a domain where the imperatives of human prosperity intersected with the imperative of environmental sustainability.

As they congregated in a sunlit auditorium, the air buzzed with anticipation. Dr. Olivia, with her sharp intellect and unwavering commitment, stepped forward to address the attentive audience.

"Welcome, esteemed colleagues, to the frontier of economic inquiry," she began, her voice carrying the gravitas of authority. "Today, we embark on a journey to explore the profound connections between human well-being and the health of our planet—a journey into the realm of ecological economics."

Marcus, his passion for innovation evident in every word, stepped forward to share his perspective. "In our pursuit of economic progress, we must not lose sight of the delicate balance between human needs and environmental sustainability," he proclaimed, his voice resonating with conviction. "Ecological economics offers us a framework through which to reconcile these seemingly conflicting imperatives, paving the way for a future where prosperity coexists harmoniously with planetary health."

Sofia, her dedication to environmental justice unwavering, added her voice to the conversation. "By centering environmental sustainability in our economic analysis, we gain insights into the ways in which our current economic systems degrade our natural world," she asserted, her voice brimming with urgency. "We must use this knowledge to advocate for policies and practices that protect our planet, preserve biodiversity, and ensure the well-being of future generations."

As the dialogue unfolded, a sense of purpose filled the room. Ideas flowed freely, perspectives expanded, and a shared vision of a more sustainable future began to take shape.

In the days and weeks that followed, Dr. Olivia, Marcus, Sofia, and their fellow scholars delved deep into the intricacies of ecological economics. They analyzed data, conducted research, and collaborated with experts from diverse fields to develop comprehensive frameworks that balanced human needs with environmental imperatives.

Their efforts yielded profound insights into the interconnectedness of human and ecological systems, the impacts of resource extraction and consumption on biodiversity and climate change, and the urgent need for transformative change.

Armed with this knowledge, they set out to advocate for policies and interventions that promoted sustainability, resilience, and equity. And as their work gained momentum, the ripple effects spread far beyond the confines of Lusaka.

Across the globe, policymakers, economists, and activists embraced the principles of ecological economics, using them to inform policies and practices that protected the planet, preserved natural resources, and ensured a thriving future for all life on Earth.

3

Chapter Three: Human Capital and Development

In the vibrant heart of Lusaka, where the city's energy pulsated through its streets, a group of scholars and visionaries had gathered at the Lusaka Chamber of Commerce. Dr. Olivia, Marcus, Sofia, and a cohort of intellectuals had convened to delve into the complexities of human capital and development—a realm where the investment in people's skills, knowledge, and well-being intersected with the pursuit of societal progress.

As they settled into the conference room, the air buzzed with anticipation. Dr. Olivia, with her sharp intellect and commanding presence, stepped forward to address the attentive audience.

"Welcome, esteemed colleagues, to a pivotal discussion in our exploration of economics," she began, her voice carrying the weight of authority. "Today, we embark on a journey to examine the critical role of human capital in fostering sustainable development—a journey into the realm where investment in people becomes the cornerstone of societal progress."

Marcus, his passion for innovation evident in every gesture, stepped forward to share his perspective. "In our quest for economic advancement, we must recognize that our greatest asset lies in the talents, skills, and creativity of our people," he proclaimed, his voice resonating with conviction. "Human capital development is not just about education and training—it's about empowering individuals to realize their full potential and contribute meaningfully to society."

Sofia, her commitment to social justice unwavering, added her voice to the conversation. "By investing in human capital, we not only enhance individual well-being but also foster inclusive growth and reduce inequality," she asserted, her voice imbued with passion. "We must ensure that everyone, regardless of background or circumstance, has access to the education, healthcare, and opportunities they need to thrive."

As the discussion unfolded, a sense of purpose filled the room. Ideas flowed freely, perspectives expanded, and a shared vision of a more equitable and prosperous society began to take shape.

In the days and weeks that followed, Dr. Olivia, Marcus, Sofia, and their fellow scholars delved deep into the intricacies of human capital and development. They analyzed data, conducted research, and collaborated with experts from diverse fields to develop comprehensive strategies for nurturing human potential and fostering sustainable progress.

Their efforts yielded profound insights into the importance of investing in education, healthcare, and social services, the impact of technological innovation on employment and skill development, and the need for policies that prioritize human well-being over short-term gains.

Armed with this knowledge, they set out to advocate for policies and interventions that promoted human capital development at all levels of society. And as their work gained momentum, the ripple effects spread far beyond the confines of Lusaka.

Across the globe, policymakers, economists, and activists embraced the principles of human capital and development, using them to inform policies and practices that empowered individuals, strengthened communities, and fostered sustainable progress for all.

The Importance of Human Capital in Economic Growth

As the discussion on human capital and development continued to unfold in the halls of the Lusaka Chamber of Commerce, Dr. Olivia, Marcus, Sofia, and their colleagues delved deeper into the critical role of human capital in driving economic growth and prosperity.

With a sense of urgency and determination, Dr. Olivia took the floor once again, her voice commanding the attention of the room.

"Human capital is the lifeblood of economic progress," she declared, her words echoing with conviction. "Investments in education, skills training, and healthcare not only enhance individual well-being but also fuel innovation, productivity, and competitiveness at the societal level."

Marcus, his eyes alight with passion and purpose, stepped forward to share his perspective. "In today's rapidly changing world, where knowledge and skills are the currency of success, human capital is more valuable than ever," he proclaimed. "By equipping people with the tools they need to adapt, innovate, and thrive, we lay the foundation for sustainable economic growth and shared prosperity."

Sofia, her commitment to social justice unwavering, added her voice to the conversation. "But we must ensure that investments in human capital are equitable and inclusive," she asserted. "Everyone, regardless of background or circumstance, deserves access to quality education, healthcare, and opportunities for personal and professional development."

As the discussion continued, a sense of clarity and purpose filled the room. Participants exchanged ideas, shared insights, and forged connections that would shape their collective understanding of the importance of human capital in driving economic growth and development.

In the days and weeks that followed, Dr. Olivia, Marcus, Sofia, and their colleagues worked tirelessly to advocate for policies and interventions that prioritized investments in human capital. They engaged with policymakers, community leaders, and the public at large, making the case for bold and transformative action to unleash the full potential of people and societies.

Their efforts did not go unnoticed. Across Lusaka and beyond, momentum grew for initiatives that expanded access to education, improved healthcare systems, and fostered environments conducive to lifelong learning and skill development.

And as their work gained traction, the ripple effects spread far beyond the confines of the conference room. Across the globe, economies flourished, communities thrived, and individuals found new opportunities for growth and fulfillment.

Education and Training as Investments in Human Capital

In the heart of Lusaka, within the hallowed halls of the Lusaka Chamber of Commerce, the discussion on human capital and development delved deeper into the transformative power of education and training as investments in human potential.

With a sense of purpose and conviction, Dr. Olivia, Marcus, Sofia, and their colleagues continued to explore the critical role of education and training in unlocking opportunities for individuals and driving economic progress for society as a whole.

Dr. Olivia, her voice steady and resolute, addressed the room once again. "Education is not just a means to acquire knowledge—it is an investment in the future," she declared, her words resonating with authority. "By equipping individuals with the skills, competencies, and critical thinking abilities they need to succeed, we empower them to reach their full potential and contribute meaningfully to society."

Marcus, his passion for innovation undimmed, stepped forward to share his perspective. "Training and skill development are essential for adapting to the demands of a rapidly changing economy," he proclaimed. "In today's knowledge-based world, where technological advancements and automation are reshaping industries, lifelong learning is not just a luxury—it's a necessity for staying competitive and relevant in the workforce."

Sofia, her commitment to social justice unwavering, added her voice to the conversation. "But we must ensure that education and training are accessible to all," she emphasized. "Too often, marginalized communities are left behind due to barriers such as lack of resources, discrimination, and systemic inequities. We must dismantle these barriers and create inclusive pathways for everyone to pursue education and skill development."

As the discussion continued, a sense of urgency and possibility filled the room. Participants exchanged ideas, shared best practices, and committed to collective action to expand access to quality education and training for all members of society.

In the days and weeks that followed, Dr. Olivia, Marcus, Sofia, and their colleagues worked tirelessly to advocate for policies and initiatives that promoted lifelong learning and skill development. They engaged with policymakers, educators, employers, and community leaders to build consensus around the importance of investing in human capital through education and training.

Their efforts bore fruit. Across Lusaka and beyond, investments in education and training surged, creating new opportunities for individuals to acquire the knowledge and skills they needed to thrive in the 21st-century economy.

And as the impact of these investments reverberated throughout society, economies flourished, innovation thrived, and social mobility soared. In the end, education and training emerged not just as tools for personal advancement, but as catalysts for societal transformation—a testament to the enduring power of human capital to drive progress and prosperity for generations to come.

Health and Well-Being: A Vital Component of Human Development

In the heart of bustling Lusaka, within the corridors of the Lusaka Chamber of Commerce, the discourse on human capital and development turned towards the critical importance of health and well-being as fundamental pillars of human development.

With unwavering determination and a shared commitment to social progress, Dr. Olivia, Marcus, Sofia, and their colleagues embarked on a journey to explore the transformative impact of prioritizing health and well-being on individual flourishing and societal advancement.

Dr. Olivia, her voice echoing with conviction, took the lead once more. "Health is not merely the absence of illness—it is the foundation upon which all human potential rests," she proclaimed. "By investing in healthcare systems, preventative measures, and public health initiatives, we not only improve individual outcomes but also lay the groundwork for sustained economic growth and social cohesion."

Marcus, his fervor for progress evident in every word, stepped forward to share his insights. "Well-being is not just a luxury reserved for the privileged—it is a fundamental human right," he asserted. "When individuals are healthy and fulfilled, they are better equipped to contribute to society, drive innovation, and participate fully in the economy."

Sofia, her compassion for the marginalized unwavering, added her voice to the discussion. "But we must ensure that access to healthcare and well-being resources is equitable and inclusive," she emphasized. "Too often, vulnerable populations are denied access to essential services due to systemic barriers and disparities. We must address these injustices and strive for a world where everyone has the opportunity to live a healthy and dignified life."

As the dialogue unfolded, a sense of urgency and solidarity permeated the room. Participants exchanged ideas, shared personal experiences, and rallied around the shared vision of a society where health and well-being were valued as paramount assets.

In the days and weeks that followed, Dr. Olivia, Marcus, Sofia, and their colleagues worked tirelessly to advocate for policies and initiatives that prioritized health and well-being as central components of human development. They collaborated with healthcare professionals, policymakers, and grassroots organizations to address systemic barriers, expand access to healthcare services, and promote mental health awareness and support.

Their efforts yielded tangible results. Across Lusaka and beyond, investments in healthcare and well-being surged, resulting in improved health outcomes, reduced healthcare disparities, and greater overall well-being for individuals and communities.

And as the impact of these investments rippled through society, economies flourished, social cohesion strengthened, and quality of life soared. In the end, health and well-being emerged not just as indicators of progress, but as fundamental rights and prerequisites for human flourishing—a testament to the transformative power of investing in the holistic development of individuals and communities alike.

Innovation and Creativity: Drivers of Human Capital Accumulation

In the heart of the bustling city of Lusaka, within the walls of the Lusaka Chamber of Commerce, the discourse on human capital and development expanded to explore the transformative role of innovation and creativity as drivers of human capital accumulation.

With a fervent desire for progress and a shared belief in the power of human ingenuity, Dr. Olivia, Marcus, Sofia, and their colleagues embarked on a journey to unlock the potential of innovation and creativity in shaping the future of society.

Dr. Olivia, her voice filled with conviction, led the discussion once again. "Innovation and creativity are the engines of progress," she declared. "By fostering environments that encourage experimentation, risk-taking, and collaboration, we can unleash the full potential of individuals and drive human capital accumulation to new heights."

Marcus, his eyes ablaze with passion, stepped forward to share his perspective. "Creativity is the currency of the future," he proclaimed. "In a rapidly changing world, where new challenges and opportunities abound, our ability to think creatively and adaptively is what sets us apart. By nurturing creativity in all its forms, we can cultivate a society where innovation thrives and human potential knows no bounds."

Sofia, her commitment to social justice unwavering, added her voice to the conversation. "But we must ensure that opportunities for innovation and creativity are accessible to all," she emphasized. "Too often, marginalized communities are excluded from the innovation ecosystem due to systemic barriers and disparities. We must break down these barriers and create pathways for everyone to contribute their unique talents and perspectives."

As the dialogue unfolded, a sense of excitement and possibility filled the room. Participants exchanged ideas, shared success stories, and envisioned a future where innovation and creativity were celebrated as core values of society.

In the days and weeks that followed, Dr. Olivia, Marcus, Sofia, and their colleagues worked tirelessly to foster a culture of innovation and creativity in Lusaka and beyond. They collaborated with entrepreneurs, artists, educators, and policymakers to create spaces for experimentation, support for risk-taking, and incentives for collaboration.

Their efforts bore fruit. Across Lusaka, innovation hubs sprung up, creative industries flourished, and a new generation of entrepreneurs and innovators emerged to tackle the pressing challenges of our time.

And as the impact of these efforts reverberated throughout society, economies thrived, communities prospered, and human capital accumulation reached new heights. In the end, innovation and creativity emerged not just as drivers of economic growth, but as catalysts for social progress and human flourishing—a testament to the transformative power of human ingenuity and imagination in shaping the destiny of nations and the lives of individuals alike.

Social Capital: Leveraging Networks for Economic Progress

In the heart of bustling Lusaka, within the halls of the Lusaka Chamber of Commerce, the discourse on human capital and development turned towards the transformative potential of social capital as a catalyst for economic progress.

With a shared commitment to fostering connections and building communities, Dr. Olivia, Marcus, Sofia, and their colleagues embarked on a journey to explore the power of social networks in driving human capital accumulation and advancing societal well-being.

Dr. Olivia, her voice resonating with purpose, took the lead once more. "Social capital is the glue that binds us together," she declared. "By nurturing strong social networks and fostering trust and reciprocity, we can unlock a wealth of opportunities for collaboration, learning, and mutual support."

Marcus, his enthusiasm infectious, stepped forward to share his insights. "In a world where relationships matter as much as resources, social capital is a key determinant of success," he proclaimed. "By leveraging our networks, we can access new markets, share knowledge and expertise, and amplify our impact far beyond what we could achieve alone."

Sofia, her compassion for the marginalized guiding her every word, added her voice to the conversation. "But we must ensure that access to social capital is equitable and inclusive," she emphasized. "Too often, marginalized communities are excluded from networks of power and influence, perpetuating cycles of disadvantage. We must work to dismantle these barriers and create spaces where everyone has the opportunity to connect, collaborate, and thrive."

As the dialogue unfolded, a sense of camaraderie and solidarity filled the room. Participants shared stories of how their own social networks had enriched their lives and expanded their horizons, underscoring the importance of social capital in driving human development and societal progress.

In the days and weeks that followed, Dr. Olivia, Marcus, Sofia, and their colleagues worked tirelessly to strengthen social capital in Lusaka and beyond. They organized networking events, facilitated mentorship programs, and fostered partnerships between businesses, community organizations, and academic institutions.

Their efforts yielded tangible results. Across Lusaka, social networks flourished, bonds strengthened, and a sense of community deepened. People from all walks of life came together to support one another, share resources, and work towards common goals.

And as the impact of these efforts reverberated throughout society, economies thrived, innovation surged, and social cohesion soared. In the end, social capital emerged not just as a concept, but as a lived reality—a testament to the power of human connections to drive economic progress and foster thriving, resilient communities for generations to come.

Policy Implications for Enhancing Human Capital Development

Within the vibrant corridors of the Lusaka Chamber of Commerce, Dr. Olivia, Marcus, Sofia, and their esteemed colleagues convened to explore the policy implications for enhancing human capital development—a pivotal discussion that would shape the future of their society.

Dr. Olivia, her voice commanding attention, addressed the assembled group. "As stewards of economic progress, it falls upon us to translate our insights into actionable policies that empower individuals, foster innovation, and drive societal advancement," she proclaimed. "Our task is to design policies that prioritize human capital development as the cornerstone of our collective prosperity."

Marcus, his eyes alight with fervor, stepped forward to offer his perspective. "Policies that promote access to education, training, and healthcare are essential," he declared. "But we must also address systemic barriers that hinder participation and perpetuate inequality. By implementing policies that ensure equitable access to opportunities for all, we can unlock the full potential of our society."

Sofia, her commitment to social justice unwavering, added her voice to the conversation. "Furthermore, we must invest in social safety nets and support systems that protect the most vulnerable among us," she asserted. "Policies that provide access to affordable housing, healthcare, and childcare are essential for fostering an environment where everyone can thrive."

As the dialogue unfolded, a sense of purpose and urgency permeated the room. Participants exchanged ideas, debated solutions, and grappled with the complexities of translating theory into practice.

In the days and weeks that followed, Dr. Olivia, Marcus, Sofia, and their colleagues worked tirelessly to develop policy recommendations that reflected their collective vision for human capital development. They engaged with policymakers, stakeholders, and the public to build consensus around their proposals and mobilize support for meaningful change.

Their efforts did not go unnoticed. Across Lusaka, policymakers embraced their recommendations, enacting legislation and initiatives aimed at expanding access to education, healthcare, and social services. Investments in infrastructure, innovation, and workforce development surged, laying the groundwork for sustained economic growth and societal advancement.

And as the impact of these policies rippled through society, economies thrived, communities prospered, and individuals flourished. In the end, the policy implications for enhancing human capital development emerged not just as a theoretical exercise, but as a blueprint for building a more equitable, resilient, and prosperous future for all.

4

Chapter Four: Inequality and Social Justice

In the heart of the bustling city of Lusaka, where the stark contrast between opulence and deprivation was a constant reminder of the deep-rooted inequalities that plagued society, a group of scholars and activists gathered at the Lusaka Chamber of Commerce to confront the pressing issues of inequality and social justice.

Led by Dr. Olivia, Marcus, Sofia, and a diverse array of voices from academia, civil society, and the grassroots, the discussion delved into the systemic barriers that perpetuated inequality and the urgent need for transformative change.

Dr. Olivia, her gaze steely and her resolve unwavering, addressed the assembled group. "Inequality is not just a matter of economics—it is a moral imperative," she declared. "As scholars and advocates, it is our duty to shine a light on the injustices that divide our society and work towards a future where every individual has the opportunity to thrive."

Marcus, his passion for justice burning brightly, stepped forward to share his perspective. "Inequality erodes the fabric of our society, breeding resentment, despair, and unrest," he proclaimed. "We cannot claim to be a just society when so many are left behind, their voices silenced by the weight of poverty and marginalization."

Sofia, her empathy for the marginalized guiding her every word, added her voice to the conversation. "But we must not despair in the face of injustice," she urged. "For every problem, there is a solution. By organizing, mobilizing, and advocating for change, we can build a more equitable and inclusive society for all."

As the dialogue unfolded, a sense of solidarity and determination filled the room. Participants shared stories of resilience, discussed strategies for action, and pledged their commitment to the fight for social justice.

In the days and weeks that followed, Dr. Olivia, Marcus, Sofia, and their colleagues worked tirelessly to address the root causes of inequality and advocate for policies and initiatives that promoted fairness, equity, and inclusion.

They engaged with policymakers, community leaders, and the public, rallying support for measures such as progressive taxation, living wages, and investments in education, healthcare, and affordable housing.

Their efforts sparked a wave of change across Lusaka. Grassroots movements emerged, demanding justice for marginalized communities and holding those in power accountable for their actions.

And as the momentum for change grew, the impact rippled far beyond the confines of the conference room. Across Lusaka and beyond, policies were enacted, institutions were reformed, and attitudes shifted towards a more equitable and just society.

Understanding Economic Inequality: Causes and Consequences

As the discussion on inequality and social justice continued to unfold within the walls of the Lusaka Chamber of Commerce, Dr. Olivia, Marcus, Sofia, and their colleagues delved deeper into the complex factors driving economic inequality and the far-reaching consequences it had on society.

With a sense of urgency and a commitment to uncovering truth, Dr. Olivia took the floor once more, her voice echoing with authority.

"Economic inequality is not a natural phenomenon—it is the result of deliberate choices and systemic injustices," she declared. "To address it effectively, we must first understand its root causes and the profound consequences it has on individuals, communities, and society as a whole."

Marcus, his determination to seek justice unwavering, stepped forward to share his insights. "The causes of economic inequality are multifaceted," he proclaimed. "From systemic racism and discrimination to unequal access to education, healthcare, and economic opportunities, there are myriad factors that contribute to the widening gap between the haves and the have-nots."

Sofia, her empathy for the marginalized guiding her every word, added her voice to the conversation. "And the consequences of economic inequality are dire," she emphasized. "It breeds social unrest, erodes trust in institutions, and undermines the fabric of our society. It perpetuates cycles of poverty and exclusion, trapping individuals and communities in a cycle of despair."

As the dialogue unfolded, a sense of urgency and determination filled the room. Participants exchanged ideas, shared insights, and grappled with the complexities of economic inequality and its far-reaching impact on society.

In the days and weeks that followed, Dr. Olivia, Marcus, Sofia, and their colleagues worked tirelessly to elevate awareness of the causes and consequences of economic inequality. They conducted research, organized workshops, and engaged with policymakers, stakeholders, and the public to build consensus around the need for bold and transformative action.

Their efforts bore fruit. Across Lusaka, conversations shifted, attitudes changed, and a growing movement for economic justice emerged. Grassroots organizations mobilized, demanding policy reforms and systemic changes to address the root causes of inequality and create a more just and equitable society for all.

And as the momentum for change continued to build, the impact rippled far beyond the confines of the conference room. Across Lusaka and beyond, policymakers took heed, enacting legislation and initiatives aimed at tackling economic inequality and leveling the playing field for all members of society.

Intersecting Inequalities; Race, Gender, Class and Beyond

As the discussion on economic inequality unfolded within the walls of the Lusaka Chamber of Commerce, Dr. Olivia, Marcus, Sofia, and their colleagues turned their attention to the intersecting inequalities that permeated society—inequalities rooted in race, gender, class, and beyond.

With a sense of urgency and a commitment to unraveling

the complexities of privilege and oppression, Dr. Olivia once again took the floor, her voice resolute.

"In our quest for social justice, we cannot ignore the intersecting inequalities that shape people's lived experiences," she declared. "Race, gender, class, and other intersecting identities intersect in ways that compound oppression and deepen the divides within our society."

Marcus, his determination to confront injustice unyielding, stepped forward to share his insights. "For too long, marginalized communities have borne the brunt of systemic discrimination and structural barriers," he proclaimed. "From racial profiling and wage gaps to barriers to upward mobility and access to resources, intersecting inequalities perpetuate cycles of disadvantage and marginalization."

Sofia, her empathy for the marginalized guiding her every word, added her voice to the conversation. "And the consequences of intersecting inequalities are profound," she emphasized. "They exacerbate social disparities, limit opportunities for advancement, and undermine the principles of fairness and equality that are supposed to underpin our society."

As the dialogue unfolded, a sense of solidarity and determination filled the room. Participants shared personal stories, exchanged insights, and grappled with the intersecting forces of oppression that shaped their world.

In the days and weeks that followed, Dr. Olivia, Marcus, Sofia, and their colleagues worked tirelessly to elevate awareness of intersecting inequalities and their impact on society. They collaborated with grassroots organizations, hosted workshops, and engaged with policymakers to advocate for policies and initiatives that addressed the root causes of oppression and discrimination.

Their efforts sparked a wave of change across Lusaka. Community-led movements emerged, demanding justice for marginalized communities and calling for systemic reforms to dismantle the intersecting barriers that perpetuated inequality and exclusion.

And as the momentum for change continued to grow, the impact rippled far beyond the confines of the conference room. Across Lusaka and beyond, conversations shifted, attitudes changed, and a new commitment to addressing intersecting inequalities took root.

Poverty and Social Exclusion: Challenges to Human Dignity

As the discourse on economic inequality unfolded within the halls of the Lusaka Chamber of Commerce, Dr. Olivia, Marcus, Sofia, and their colleagues shifted their focus to the harrowing realities of poverty and social exclusion—challenges that struck at the very core of human dignity.

With a sense of urgency and compassion, Dr. Olivia once again took center stage, her voice carrying the weight of empathy and determination.

"Poverty and social exclusion are not just statistical data—they are lived experiences that strip individuals of their dignity and agency," she declared, her words resonating with a profound sense of empathy. "In our pursuit of social justice, it is imperative that we confront the root causes of poverty and address the systemic barriers that perpetuate social exclusion."

Marcus, his resolve to combat injustice unshakable, stepped forward to share his insights. "For those trapped in the cycle of poverty, every day is a battle for survival—a struggle against hunger, homelessness, and despair," he proclaimed. "Social exclusion further compounds their suffering, denying them access to essential services, opportunities for advancement, and a sense of belonging in society."

Sofia, her commitment to uplifting the marginalized unwavering, added her voice to the conversation. "But poverty is not just a matter of economic deprivation—it is a violation of human dignity," she emphasized. "It robs individuals of their potential, their dreams, and their right to live a life of dignity and respect."

As the dialogue unfolded, a sense of solidarity and empathy filled the room. Participants shared stories of resilience, discussed strategies for action, and reaffirmed their commitment to standing in solidarity with those affected by poverty and social exclusion.

In the days and weeks that followed, Dr. Olivia, Marcus, Sofia, and their colleagues worked tirelessly to confront poverty and social exclusion head-on. They collaborated with grassroots organizations, mobilized resources, and advocated for policies and initiatives that addressed the root causes of poverty and promoted social inclusion.

Their efforts sparked a wave of change across Lusaka. Communities rallied together, offering support to those in need, and challenging the structures of inequality that perpetuated poverty and exclusion.

And as the momentum for change continued to grow, the impact rippled far beyond the confines of the conference room. Across Lusaka and beyond, conversations shifted, attitudes changed, and a new commitment to ending poverty and promoting social inclusion took root.

Redistribution Policies: Addressing Inequality Through Economic Measures

As the discourse on economic inequality continued to unfold within the halls of the Lusaka Chamber of Commerce, Dr. Olivia, Marcus, Sofia, and their colleagues turned their attention to the critical role of redistribution policies in addressing inequality and promoting social justice.

With a sense of purpose and a commitment to systemic change, Dr. Olivia once again took the lead, her voice ringing with determination.

"Redistribution policies are not just about wealth transfer—they are about restoring balance, fairness, and dignity to our society," she declared, her words echoing through the room. "By implementing measures that redistribute resources and opportunities more equitably, we can uplift the marginalized, narrow the gap between the rich and the poor, and create a more just and inclusive society for all."

Marcus, his passion for economic justice undimmed, stepped forward to share his insights. "Redistribution policies have the power to level the playing field and ensure that everyone has access to the resources they need to thrive," he proclaimed. "From progressive taxation and social welfare programs to universal basic income and wealth redistribution initiatives, there are myriad tools at our disposal to address the root causes of inequality and promote economic security for all."

Sofia, her commitment to social equity guiding her every word, added her voice to the conversation. "But redistribution policies must be designed with equity and inclusion in mind," she emphasized. "We must ensure that they are targeted towards those who need them most, and that they do not inadvertently perpetuate existing disparities or marginalize vulnerable communities further."

As the dialogue unfolded, a sense of urgency and possibility filled the room. Participants exchanged ideas, debated solutions, and grappled with the complexities of implementing effective redistribution policies in a diverse and interconnected society.

In the days and weeks that followed, Dr. Olivia, Marcus, Sofia, and their colleagues worked tirelessly to advocate for the implementation of redistribution policies that addressed the root causes of inequality and promoted social justice.

They engaged with policymakers, stakeholders, and the public, building consensus around the need for bold and transformative action. Grassroots movements emerged, demanding justice for marginalized communities and holding those in power accountable for their actions.

And as the momentum for change continued to build, the impact rippled far beyond the confines of the conference room. Across Lusaka and beyond, policymakers took heed, enacting legislation and initiatives aimed at redistributing wealth and resources more equitably, and ensuring that everyone had the opportunity to live with dignity, respect, and economic security.

Social Justice Movements: Advocating for Fairness and Equity

In the heart of the bustling city of Lusaka, within the walls of the Lusaka Chamber of Commerce, the discussion on economic inequality expanded to explore the pivotal role of social justice movements in advocating for fairness and equity in society.

With a shared commitment to challenging the status quo and championing the rights of the marginalized, Dr. Olivia, Marcus, Sofia, and their colleagues delved into the transformative power of grassroots activism and collective action.

Dr. Olivia, her voice filled with conviction, addressed the assembled group once more. "Social justice movements are the lifeblood of our society—they are the voices of the marginalized, the champions of the oppressed, and the catalysts for change," she proclaimed. "Through their tireless advocacy and unwavering commitment to justice, they have the power to challenge entrenched power structures, shift societal norms, and drive meaningful progress towards a more equitable and inclusive future."

Marcus, his passion for social change palpable, stepped forward to share his insights. "Social justice movements are not just about protesting—they are about organizing, mobilizing, and building power from the ground up," he declared. "They give voice to those who have been silenced by oppression, and they hold those in power accountable for their actions."

Sofia, her dedication to uplifting the marginalized guiding her every word, added her voice to the conversation. "But social justice movements are not monolithic—they are diverse, intersectional, and inclusive," she emphasized. "They recognize the interconnectedness of oppression and privilege, and they strive to create spaces where everyone's voice is heard and valued."

As the dialogue unfolded, a sense of solidarity and determination filled the room. Participants shared stories of resilience, discussed strategies for action, and reaffirmed their commitment to standing in solidarity with social justice movements.

In the days and weeks that followed, Dr. Olivia, Marcus, Sofia, and their colleagues worked tirelessly to support social justice movements and amplify their voices. They marched in solidarity, provided resources and training, and leveraged their platforms to raise awareness of pressing social issues.

Their efforts sparked a wave of change across Lusaka. Grassroots movements flourished, demanding justice for marginalized communities and challenging the structures of power and privilege that perpetuated inequality and oppression.

And as the momentum for change continued to grow, the impact rippled far beyond the confines of the conference room. Across Lusaka and beyond, social justice movements reshaped the discourse, influenced policy decisions, and inspired a new generation of activists to join the fight for a more just and equitable society.

Building Inclusive Economies: Strategies for Reducing Disparities

Within the hallowed halls of the Lusaka Chamber of Commerce, the discourse on economic inequality evolved to explore strategies for building inclusive economies and reducing disparities that plagued society. Dr. Olivia, Marcus, Sofia, and their esteemed colleagues gathered once more, their minds focused on the task at hand.

Dr. Olivia, her voice resonating with determination, addressed the assembled group. "Building inclusive economies is not just a moral imperative—it is essential for sustainable development and societal well-being," she declared. "By implementing strategies that prioritize equity and inclusion, we can create economies that work for everyone, not just the privileged few."

Marcus, his commitment to economic justice unwavering, stepped forward to share his insights. "Inclusive economies are built on the principle of shared prosperity," he proclaimed. "By investing in education, job training, and entrepreneurship programs, we can empower individuals from all walks of life to participate in and benefit from economic opportunities."

Sofia, her compassion for the marginalized guiding her every word, added her voice to the conversation. "But building inclusive economies requires more than just economic policies—it requires a fundamental shift in mindset and culture," she emphasized. "We must challenge the entrenched biases and discriminatory practices that perpetuate inequality and exclusion, and create environments where diversity and inclusion are celebrated and valued."

As the dialogue unfolded, a sense of urgency and possibility filled the room. Participants exchanged ideas, debated solutions, and grappled with the complexities of building inclusive economies in a rapidly changing world.

In the days and weeks that followed, Dr. Olivia, Marcus, Sofia, and their colleagues worked tirelessly to advance strategies for reducing disparities and promoting inclusion in Lusaka and beyond. They collaborated with policymakers, business leaders, and community organizations to develop innovative solutions and implement policies that fostered economic opportunity for all.

Their efforts bore fruit. Across Lusaka, initiatives were launched to support marginalized communities, promote diversity and inclusion in the workplace, and create pathways to economic mobility for those left behind by traditional economic systems.

5

Chapter Five: Human-Centered Business Practices

In the heart of the bustling city of Lusaka, where Buildings gleamed in the sunlight and the pulse of commerce filled the air, a new chapter began to unfold at the Lusaka Chamber of Commerce. Dr. Olivia, Marcus, Sofia, and their colleagues gathered once more, their minds alight with the promise of human-centered business practices.

With a shared vision of redefining the role of business in society and prioritizing the well-being of people over profit, they embarked on a journey to explore the transformative potential of human-centered approaches to commerce.

Dr. Olivia, her voice filled with conviction, addressed the assembled group. "Human-centered business practices are not just about maximizing profits—they are about creating value for all stakeholders, from employees and customers to communities and the environment," she declared. "By prioritizing human well-being and sustainability, businesses can drive meaningful impact and build a better world for future generations."

Marcus, his passion for ethical entrepreneurship burning brightly, stepped forward to share his insights. "In a world where corporate greed and short-term thinking often prevail, human-centered businesses stand out as beacons of hope and integrity," he proclaimed. "By fostering a culture of empathy, collaboration, and social responsibility, they can drive innovation, build trust, and create lasting value for society."

Sofia, her commitment to social justice guiding her every word, added her voice to the conversation. "But human-centered business practices must go beyond lip service—they must be embedded in the DNA of organizations, from their mission statements and corporate policies to their day-to-day operations and decision-making processes," she emphasized. "Only then can we truly harness the power of business as a force for good in the world."

As the dialogue unfolded, a sense of possibility and purpose filled the room. Participants exchanged ideas, shared best practices, and grappled with the complexities of implementing human-centered business practices in a competitive and profit-driven landscape.

In the days and weeks that followed, Dr. Olivia, Marcus, Sofia, and their colleagues worked tirelessly to champion human-centered approaches to business. They collaborated with industry leaders, hosted workshops, and conducted research to advance the principles of empathy, sustainability, and social responsibility in the business world.

Their efforts sparked a wave of change across Lusaka and beyond. Businesses embraced human-centered practices, adopting policies and initiatives that prioritized employee well-being, customer satisfaction, and environmental stewardship.

And as the impact of these efforts rippled through society, a new paradigm of business emerged—one where profit and purpose coexisted harmoniously, and where businesses served as catalysts for positive social and environmental change.

Corporate Social Responsibility: Beyond Profit Maximization

As the discussion on human-centered business practices continued to unfold at the Lusaka Chamber of Commerce, Dr. Olivia, Marcus, Sofia, and their colleagues delved into the critical importance of corporate social responsibility (CSR) as a cornerstone of ethical business conduct.

With a shared commitment to redefining the role of corporations in society and prioritizing the well-being of people and the planet, they explored the transformative potential of CSR in driving positive impact and creating value beyond profit maximization.

Dr. Olivia, her voice resonating with conviction, addressed the assembled group once more. "Corporate social responsibility is not just a buzzword—it is a moral imperative for businesses in the 21st century," she declared. "By embracing CSR, companies can align their interests with those of society, mitigate risks, and build trust and goodwill among their stakeholders."

Marcus, his dedication to ethical entrepreneurship unwavering, stepped forward to share his insights. "In a world where the actions of corporations can have far-reaching consequences, CSR offers a pathway to responsible and sustainable business practices," he proclaimed. "By integrating social and environmental considerations into their decision-making processes, companies can create shared value for all stakeholders and contribute to the greater good."

Sofia, her passion for social justice guiding her every word, added her voice to the conversation. "But CSR must go beyond mere philanthropy—it must be integrated into the core business strategy and operations of companies," she emphasized. "From ethical sourcing and fair labor practices to environmental sustainability and community engagement, CSR encompasses a wide range of initiatives that can drive positive change and make a meaningful difference in the world."

As the dialogue unfolded, a sense of purpose and possibility filled the room. Participants exchanged ideas, shared best practices, and grappled with the complexities of implementing CSR in a competitive business landscape.

In the days and weeks that followed, Dr. Olivia, Marcus, Sofia, and their colleagues worked tirelessly to advocate for the adoption of CSR principles and practices in the business community. They collaborated with industry leaders, engaged with policymakers, and mobilized public support to advance the cause of responsible and sustainable business conduct.

Their efforts bore fruit. Across Lusaka and beyond, companies embraced CSR as a guiding principle, implementing policies and initiatives that promoted social responsibility, environmental stewardship, and ethical governance.

And as the impact of these efforts rippled through society, businesses became agents of positive change, driving innovation, fostering inclusivity, and contributing to the well-being of people and the planet.

CHAPTER FIVE: HUMAN-CENTERED BUSINESS PRACTICES

Ethical Leadership: Fostering a Culture of Integrity in Organizations

Within the walls of the Lusaka Chamber of Commerce, the discussion on human-centered business practices continued to unfold, with a particular focus on the pivotal role of ethical leadership in fostering a culture of integrity within organizations.

With a shared commitment to re-imagining the dynamics of power and influence in the corporate world, Dr. Olivia, Marcus, Sofia, and their colleagues delved into the transformative potential of ethical leadership in shaping organizational culture and driving positive change.

Dr. Olivia, her voice infused with gravitas, addressed the assembled group once more. "Ethical leadership is the cornerstone of a healthy and sustainable organization," she declared. "By leading with integrity, empathy, and transparency, leaders can inspire trust, foster collaboration, and create an environment where employees feel valued, respected, and empowered to do their best work."

Marcus, his dedication to principled leadership unwavering, stepped forward to share his insights. "In a world where corporate scandals and ethical lapses abound, ethical leadership offers a beacon of hope and accountability," he proclaimed. "By setting a clear example and holding themselves and others to the highest standards of ethical conduct, leaders can cultivate a culture of integrity that permeates every aspect of the organization."

Sofia, her commitment to social justice guiding her every word, added her voice to the conversation. "But ethical leadership is not just about following the rules—it's about doing what's right, even when it's difficult or unpopular," she emphasized. "It's about standing up for justice, championing diversity and inclusion, and holding ourselves accountable for the impact of our actions on others and the world around us."

As the dialogue unfolded, a sense of responsibility and resolve filled the room. Participants exchanged ideas, shared personal anecdotes, and grappled with the complexities of ethical leadership in a rapidly evolving business landscape.

In the days and weeks that followed, Dr. Olivia, Marcus, Sofia, and their colleagues worked tirelessly to promote the principles of ethical leadership within organizations. They offered training and development programs, facilitated discussions on ethical dilemmas, and provided guidance and support to leaders at all levels.

Their efforts sparked a wave of change across Lusaka and beyond. Companies embraced ethical leadership as a core value, appointing leaders who embodied integrity, empathy, and a commitment to doing what's right.

And as the impact of these efforts rippled through organizations, a new era of ethical leadership emerged—one where leaders led by example, inspired trust, and fostered a culture of integrity that empowered employees to act with courage, compassion, and conviction.

Stakeholder Engagement: Balancing the Needs of Various Interest Groups

In the vibrant hub of the Lusaka Chamber of Commerce, the discourse on human-centered business practices evolved to explore the intricate dance of stakeholder engagement—the delicate art of balancing the needs and interests of various groups within and outside organizations.

With a shared commitment to fostering collaboration, inclusivity, and mutual respect, Dr. Olivia, Marcus, Sofia, and their colleagues delved into the transformative potential of stakeholder engagement in building sustainable and resilient organizations.

Dr. Olivia, her voice resonating with wisdom, addressed the assembled group once more. "Stakeholder engagement is the cornerstone of effective decision-making and responsible governance," she declared. "By actively involving stakeholders in the decision-making process, organizations can gain valuable insights, build trust, and create shared value for all involved."

Marcus, his dedication to inclusive leadership unwavering, stepped forward to share his insights. "In a world where the actions of organizations can have far-reaching consequences, stakeholder engagement offers a pathway to accountability and transparency," he proclaimed. "By listening to the voices of stakeholders and considering their perspectives, organizations can make more informed decisions that reflect the diverse needs and interests of their stakeholders."

Sofia, her commitment to social justice guiding her every word, added her voice to the conversation. "But stakeholder engagement must go beyond mere consultation—it must be meaningful, inclusive, and empowering," she emphasized. "It's about building relationships based on trust and mutual respect, and co-creating solutions that address the root causes of issues and create positive change."

As the dialogue unfolded, a sense of collaboration and empathy filled the room. Participants exchanged ideas, shared experiences, and grappled with the complexities of stakeholder engagement in a dynamic and interconnected world.

In the days and weeks that followed, Dr. Olivia, Marcus, Sofia, and their colleagues worked tirelessly to champion stakeholder engagement within organizations. They facilitated dialogue sessions, conducted surveys, and organized community forums to ensure that the voices of stakeholders were heard and valued.

Their efforts sparked a wave of change across Lusaka and beyond. Organizations embraced stakeholder engagement as a core principle, integrating it into their decision-making processes and governance structures.

And as the impact of these efforts rippled through organizations, a new era of stakeholder engagement emerged—one where organizations worked collaboratively with stakeholders to address complex challenges, foster innovation, and drive positive social and environmental impact.

Employee Well-being: Creating Supportive Work Environments

Within the bustling corridors of the Lusaka Chamber of Commerce, the discourse on human-centered business practices took a poignant turn towards the vital importance of prioritizing employee well-being and fostering supportive work environments within organizations.

With a shared dedication to nurturing the holistic health and happiness of employees, Dr. Olivia, Marcus, Sofia, and their esteemed colleagues delved into the transformative potential of creating workplaces where individuals could thrive, both personally and professionally.

Dr. Olivia, her voice filled with compassion, addressed the assembled group once more. "Employee well-being is not just a matter of productivity—it's a fundamental human right," she declared. "By prioritizing the physical, mental, and emotional health of employees, organizations can create environments where individuals feel valued, respected, and empowered to bring their whole selves to work."

Marcus, his commitment to compassionate leadership unwavering, stepped forward to share his insights. "In a world where burnout and stress are all too common, employee well-being offers a pathway to resilience and fulfillment," he proclaimed. "By fostering a culture of care, support, and work-life balance, organizations can unleash the full potential of their employees and drive sustainable performance and growth."

Sofia, her empathy for the workforce guiding her every word, added her voice to the conversation. "But employee well-being must go beyond superficial perks—it must be ingrained in the fabric of organizational culture and practices," she emphasized. "It's about creating psychological safety, fostering a sense of belonging, and providing resources and support for employees to thrive in all aspects of their lives."

As the dialogue unfolded, a sense of empathy and solidarity filled the room. Participants shared personal stories, exchanged best practices, and grappled with the complexities of supporting employee well-being in a fast-paced and competitive business environment.

In the days and weeks that followed, Dr. Olivia, Marcus, Sofia, and their colleagues worked tirelessly to advocate for the prioritization of employee well-being within organizations. They championed flexible work arrangements, promoted mental health awareness, and encouraged leaders to lead by example in prioritizing self-care and work-life balance.

Their efforts sparked a wave of change across Lusaka and beyond. Organizations embraced a holistic approach to employee well-being, implementing initiatives such as wellness programs, mindfulness training, and employee assistance programs to support the physical, mental, and emotional health of their workforce.

And as the impact of these efforts rippled through organizations, a new era of supportive work environments emerged—one where employees felt valued, empowered, and supported to bring their best selves to work each day.

Sustainable Business Models; Integrating Environmental and Social Considerations

Amidst the vibrant discussions at the Lusaka Chamber of Commerce, the exploration of human-centered business practices expanded to encompass the imperative of sustainable business models—ones that seamlessly integrated environmental and social considerations into their core operations.

With a shared commitment to stewarding the planet and serving communities, Dr. Olivia, Marcus, Sofia, and their esteemed colleagues delved into the transformative potential of embracing sustainability as a guiding principle in business.

Dr. Olivia, her voice resonating with urgency, addressed the gathered audience once more. "Sustainable business models are not just a trend—they are a necessity in an era defined by environmental degradation and social inequality," she declared. "By prioritizing environmental conservation and social responsibility, organizations can create long-term value while safeguarding the planet and promoting human well-being."

Marcus, his dedication to ethical entrepreneurship unwavering, stepped forward to share his insights. "In a world where natural resources are finite and social injustices abound, sustainable business models offer a path forward," he proclaimed. "By embracing principles of circularity, resource efficiency, and social equity, businesses can minimize their environmental footprint and maximize their positive impact on society."

Sofia, her commitment to environmental justice guiding her every word, added her voice to the conversation. "But sustainable business models must go beyond mere tokenism—they must be deeply integrated into the DNA of organizations," she emphasized. "It's about re-imagining business practices, supply chains, and value chains to ensure that they are regenerative, inclusive, and aligned with the needs of both people and the planet."

As the dialogue unfolded, a sense of responsibility and possibility filled the room. Participants shared success stories, exchanged innovative ideas, and grappled with the complexities of transitioning to sustainable business models in a world grappling with climate change and social inequity.

In the days and weeks that followed, Dr. Olivia, Marcus, Sofia, and their colleagues worked tirelessly to advocate for the adoption of sustainable business practices within organizations. They collaborated with industry leaders, engaged with policymakers, and mobilized public support to advance the cause of sustainability in business.

Their efforts sparked a wave of change across Lusaka and beyond. Companies embraced sustainable business models as a strategic imperative, implementing initiatives such as renewable energy adoption, waste reduction, and fair labor practices to minimize their environmental impact and maximize their social value.

And as the impact of these efforts rippled through organizations, a new era of sustainable business emerged—one where profit and purpose were not mutually exclusive, but intricately intertwined in a virtuous cycle of prosperity and progress.

Responsible Consumption and Production: Empowering Consumers for Positive Change

In the lively halls of the Lusaka Chamber of Commerce, the conversation on human-centered business practices delved deeper into the imperative of responsible consumption and production—empowering consumers to drive positive change through their purchasing choices.

With a shared commitment to fostering sustainability and social responsibility, Dr. Olivia, Marcus, Sofia, and their esteemed colleagues explored the transformative potential of educating and empowering consumers to make informed and ethical decisions.

Dr. Olivia, her voice filled with determination, addressed the assembled group once more. "Responsible consumption and production are not just about what we buy—they're about the impact of our choices on the planet and society," she declared. "By empowering consumers with knowledge and awareness, we can catalyze a shift towards more sustainable and ethical practices throughout the supply chain."

Marcus, his dedication to ethical entrepreneurship unwavering, stepped forward to share his insights. "In a world where consumerism drives much of our economy, responsible consumption is a powerful tool for change," he proclaimed. "By choosing products and brands that align with our values, we can send a clear message to businesses that sustainability and social responsibility matter."

Sofia, her commitment to environmental justice guiding her every word, added her voice to the conversation. "But responsible consumption goes beyond individual actions—it's about collective impact," she emphasized. "By organizing campaigns, advocating for transparency, and holding companies accountable for their practices, consumers can amplify their voices and drive systemic change."

As the dialogue unfolded, a sense of empowerment and possibility filled the room. Participants shared stories of conscious consumerism, exchanged tips for sustainable living, and grappled with the complexities of navigating a consumer landscape dominated by fast fashion, disposable products, and unethical practices.

In the days and weeks that followed, Dr. Olivia, Marcus, Sofia, and their colleagues worked tirelessly to educate and empower consumers to make more responsible choices. They hosted workshops, launched awareness campaigns, and collaborated with community organizations to promote sustainable consumption and production practices.

Their efforts sparked a wave of change across Lusaka and beyond. Consumers became more conscious of the impact of their purchasing decisions, demanding transparency and accountability from businesses and driving demand for ethically sourced, environmentally friendly products.

And as the impact of these efforts rippled through society, a new era of responsible consumption and production emerged—one where consumers wielded their purchasing power as a force for good, driving positive change and shaping a more sustainable and equitable future for all.

6

Chapter Six: Globalization's Impact on Human Welfare: Opportunities and Challenges

In the halls of the Lusaka Chamber of Commerce, the discussion turned to the complex phenomenon of globalization and its profound implications for human welfare—unveiling both promising opportunities and daunting challenges for societies around the world.

Dr. Olivia, Marcus, Sofia, and their esteemed colleagues gathered once more, their minds ablaze with the intricacies of this global force reshaping the economic landscape.

Dr. Olivia, her voice echoing with insight, addressed the assembled group. "Globalization has ushered in an era of unprecedented interconnectedness, offering immense opportunities for economic growth, innovation, and cultural exchange," she declared. "But alongside these opportunities come significant challenges, including widening income inequality, environmental degradation, and the erosion of local cultures and traditions."

Marcus, his gaze fixed on the horizon of global markets, stepped forward to share his perspectives. "For entrepreneurs like us, globalization opens doors to new markets, technologies, and ideas," he proclaimed. "But it also presents hurdles such as fierce competition, supply chain disruptions, and the exploitation of labor and resources in pursuit of profit."

Sofia, her compassion for the marginalized driving her words, added her voice to the dialogue. "Globalization has led to the displacement of workers, the marginalization of vulnerable communities, and the concentration of wealth in the hands of a few," she emphasized. "But it also offers opportunities for collaboration, solidarity, and collective action to address global challenges and build a more just and equitable world."

As the discourse unfolded, a tapestry of perspectives emerged, weaving together the complexities of globalization's impact on human welfare—illuminating its multifaceted nature and the need for nuanced responses.

In the days and weeks that followed, Dr. Olivia, Marcus, Sofia, and their colleagues delved deeper into the opportunities and challenges of globalization, exploring strategies to harness its potential for the greater good while mitigating its negative consequences.

They collaborated with international organizations, conducted research on global trends, and engaged with policymakers to advocate for policies that promote inclusive growth, environmental sustainability, and social justice in an increasingly interconnected world.

Their efforts sparked a renewed sense of urgency and purpose, inspiring individuals and communities to come together across borders and boundaries to tackle shared challenges and seize collective opportunities.

And as the impact of globalization continued to unfold, a new vision emerged—one where the benefits of global interconnectedness were equitably shared, and the dignity and well-being of all people were safeguarded in a truly global community.

Globalization and Human Development

As the discussion on globalization's impact on human welfare continued to unfold at the Lusaka Chamber of Commerce, the focus shifted towards the intersection of globalization and human development—an exploration of how this global force shapes the well-being and opportunities of individuals and societies around the world.

Dr. Olivia, Marcus, Sofia, and their esteemed colleagues reconvened, their minds alight with the complexities of this critical subpoint.

Dr. Olivia, her voice filled with insight, addressed the gathering once more. "Globalization has the potential to accelerate human development by expanding access to markets, knowledge, and technology," she declared. "But it also poses challenges such as widening disparities, cultural homogenization, and the erosion of local identities."

Marcus, his eyes alight with passion for progress, stepped forward to share his perspective. "For entrepreneurs and innovators, globalization offers unprecedented opportunities to collaborate across borders, tap into global markets, and access resources and talent from around the world," he proclaimed. "But it also requires navigating complex regulatory environments, cultural differences, and geopolitical risks."

Sofia, her heart attuned to the plight of the marginalized, added her voice to the conversation. "Globalization has the potential to exacerbate inequalities, marginalize vulnerable populations, and undermine local economies," she emphasized. "But it also presents opportunities for solidarity, cooperation, and mutual support to address shared challenges and advance human development for all."

As the dialogue unfolded, a tapestry of perspectives emerged, weaving together the nuanced dynamics of globalization's impact on human development—illuminating both its promise and its pitfalls.

In the days and weeks that followed, Dr. Olivia, Marcus, Sofia, and their colleagues delved deeper into the complexities of globalization and human development, exploring strategies to maximize its benefits while mitigating its negative consequences.

They engaged with international development agencies, conducted research on global trends, and collaborated with grassroots organizations to promote policies and practices that fostered inclusive growth, social equity, and sustainable development in an increasingly interconnected world.

Their efforts sparked a renewed sense of purpose and solidarity, inspiring individuals and communities to come together across borders and boundaries to tackle shared challenges and seize collective opportunities.

And as the impact of globalization continued to unfold, a new vision emerged—one where human development was not just measured in economic terms, but in the dignity, well-being, and empowerment of all people, regardless of their background or circumstance.

In the corridors of the Lusaka Chamber of Commerce, the

conversation on globalization's impact on human welfare continued to unfold, delving deeper into the intricate web of opportunities and challenges it presents for individuals and societies worldwide.

Dr. Olivia, Marcus, Sofia, and their esteemed colleagues reconvened, their minds ablaze with the complexities of this global force shaping the economic landscape.

Dr. Olivia, her voice resonating with wisdom, addressed the assembled group once more. "Globalization offers unprecedented opportunities for economic growth, innovation, and cultural exchange," she declared. "But with these opportunities come significant challenges, including widening income inequality, environmental degradation, and the erosion of local cultures and traditions."

Marcus, his eyes alight with entrepreneurial fervor, stepped forward to share his perspective. "For entrepreneurs like us, globalization opens doors to new markets, technologies, and ideas," he proclaimed. "But it also presents hurdles such as fierce competition, supply chain disruptions, and the exploitation of labor and resources in pursuit of profit."

Sofia, her heart attuned to social justice, added her voice to the dialogue. "Globalization has led to the displacement of workers, the marginalization of vulnerable communities, and the concentration of wealth in the hands of a few," she emphasized. "But it also offers opportunities for collaboration, solidarity, and collective action to address global challenges and build a more just and equitable world."

As the discourse unfolded, a tapestry of perspectives emerged, weaving together the intricate dynamics of globalization's impact on human welfare—illuminating its multifaceted nature and the need for nuanced responses.

In the days and weeks that followed, Dr. Olivia, Marcus, Sofia, and their colleagues delved deeper into the opportunities and challenges of globalization, exploring strategies to harness its potential for the greater good while mitigating its negative consequences.

They collaborated with international organizations, conducted research on global trends, and engaged with policymakers to advocate for policies that promote inclusive growth, environmental sustainability, and social justice in an increasingly interconnected world.

Their efforts sparked a renewed sense of urgency and purpose, inspiring individuals and communities to come together across borders and boundaries to tackle shared challenges and seize collective opportunities.

And as the impact of globalization continued to unfold, a new vision emerged—one where the benefits of global interconnectedness were equitably shared, and the dignity and well-being of all people were safeguarded in a truly global community.

Trade and Economic Development: Lessons from Global Markets

As the discussion at the Lusaka Chamber of Commerce delved deeper into globalization's impact on human welfare, the spotlight shifted towards the intricate dance between trade and economic development, unveiling valuable lessons from global markets and their effects on societies worldwide.

Dr. Olivia, Marcus, Sofia, and their esteemed colleagues reconvened, their minds ignited with the complexities of this pivotal subpoint.

Dr. Olivia, her voice infused with scholarly insight, addressed the assembled group once more. "Trade has long been heralded as a catalyst for economic development, enabling countries to specialize in their comparative advantages and participate in global value chains," she declared. "Yet, it also poses challenges such as uneven distribution of gains, vulnerability to market fluctuations, and dependence on external forces."

Marcus, his entrepreneurial spirit undimmed, stepped forward to share his experiences. "For businesses, trade opens up vast opportunities to access new markets, expand their customer base, and drive innovation," he proclaimed. "However, it also demands adaptability, resilience, and strategic foresight to navigate the complexities of international competition and regulatory environments."

Sofia, her compassion for the marginalized guiding her words, added her voice to the dialogue. "Trade can be a double-edged sword, amplifying disparities and exacerbating vulnerabilities for the most marginalized communities," she emphasized. "Yet, it also offers opportunities for empowerment, capacity-building, and inclusive growth when coupled with policies that prioritize social protection, environmental sustainability, and equitable distribution of benefits."

As the discourse unfolded, a rich tapestry of perspectives emerged, weaving together the intricate dynamics of trade and economic development—illuminating both its promise and its pitfalls.

In the days and weeks that followed, Dr. Olivia, Marcus, Sofia, and their colleagues delved deeper into the lessons gleaned from global markets, exploring strategies to harness the potential of trade for sustainable and inclusive development.

They engaged with policymakers, conducted research on best practices, and collaborated with industry stakeholders to advocate for policies that fostered fair trade, empowered local producers, and protected the rights and livelihoods of workers.

Their efforts sparked a renewed sense of collaboration and solidarity, inspiring individuals and communities to come together to leverage the opportunities of trade for shared prosperity and well-being.

And as the impact of globalization continued to unfold, a new vision emerged—one where trade was not just a means of economic exchange, but a pathway to human development, dignity, and empowerment for all.

Labor Migration and Human Capital Flows

As the discussion at the Lusaka Chamber of Commerce unfolded, the focus shifted towards the complex dynamics of labor migration and human capital flows—a critical subpoint in understanding globalization's impact on human welfare.

Dr. Olivia, Marcus, Sofia, and their esteemed colleagues reconvened, their minds brimming with the intricacies of this vital aspect of global economic integration.

Dr. Olivia, her voice tinged with scholarly insight, addressed the assembled group once more. "Labor migration has become a defining feature of globalization, offering opportunities for individuals to seek better livelihoods and for economies to fill skill gaps and spur economic growth," she declared. "Yet, it also presents challenges such as brain drain, exploitation of migrant workers, and social tensions in host communities."

Marcus, his entrepreneurial acumen sharpened by global perspectives, stepped forward to share his reflections. "For businesses, labor migration provides access to a diverse talent pool, fosters innovation, and drives competitiveness," he proclaimed. "However, it also requires responsible recruitment practices, investment in skills development, and support for migrant workers' integration and well-being to ensure mutual benefits for all."

Sofia, her empathy for migrant communities guiding her words, added her voice to the dialogue. "Labor migration can be a source of empowerment and economic opportunity for individuals and families, enabling them to escape poverty, build resilience, and contribute to the development of both sending and receiving countries," she emphasized. "But it also demands protection of migrant rights, promotion of social inclusion, and recognition of their contributions to host societies."

As the discourse unfolded, a nuanced understanding of labor migration and human capital flows emerged, weaving together the complexities of mobility, opportunity, and social justice in an interconnected world.

In the days and weeks that followed, Dr. Olivia, Marcus, Sofia, and their colleagues delved deeper into the implications of labor migration, exploring strategies to maximize its benefits while mitigating its risks.

They engaged with policymakers, conducted research on migration trends, and collaborated with civil society organizations to advocate for policies that safeguarded migrant rights, promoted social cohesion, and maximized the positive impact of human capital flows on both origin and destination countries.

Their efforts sparked a renewed commitment to solidarity and cooperation, inspiring individuals and communities to come together to address the challenges and harness the opportunities of labor migration for shared prosperity and well-being.

And as the impact of globalization continued to unfold, a new vision emerged—one where labor migration was not just seen as a transactional exchange of skills, but as a transformative force for human development, dignity, and solidarity across borders.

Transnational Corporations: Balancing Profit with Social Responsibility

As the discussion at the Lusaka Chamber of Commerce unfolded, the spotlight shifted towards the role of transnational corporations (TNCs) and the delicate balance between profit-seeking and social responsibility in the globalized economy.

Dr. Olivia, Marcus, Sofia, and their esteemed colleagues reconvened, their minds ablaze with the complexities of this pivotal subpoint.

Dr. Olivia, her voice infused with scholarly insight, addressed the assembled group once more. "Transnational corporations wield immense economic power in the globalized world, driving innovation, investment, and job creation," she declared. "Yet, they also face scrutiny for their environmental impact, labor practices, and contributions to widening income inequality."

Marcus, his entrepreneurial spirit undimmed, stepped forward to share his perspective. "For businesses, profitability is paramount, but it must be balanced with social responsibility," he proclaimed. "By adopting sustainable business practices, respecting human rights, and engaging with local communities, TNCs can create shared value and contribute to the well-being of societies in which they operate."

Sofia, her heart attuned to social justice, added her voice to the dialogue. "Transnational corporations have a responsibility to uphold human rights, protect the environment, and promote social inclusion," she emphasized. "But they must also be held accountable for any harm they cause and actively work to address systemic inequalities and injustices in the global economy."

As the discourse unfolded, a tapestry of perspectives emerged, weaving together the intricate dynamics of corporate responsibility in a globalized world—illuminating both the potential for positive impact and the imperative for ethical business practices.

In the days and weeks that followed, Dr. Olivia, Marcus, Sofia, and their colleagues delved deeper into the responsibilities of TNCs, exploring strategies to promote corporate accountability and sustainability.

They engaged with stakeholders, conducted research on corporate best practices, and collaborated with advocacy groups to push for greater transparency, accountability, and respect for human rights in corporate operations.

Their efforts sparked a renewed sense of urgency and purpose, inspiring individuals and communities to come together to hold corporations accountable for their actions and advocate for a more just and equitable global economy.

And as the impact of globalization continued to unfold, a new vision emerged—one where transnational corporations operated not just for profit, but for the betterment of society and the planet, leaving a positive legacy for future generations.

International Aid and Development Assistance: Promoting Human Development Goals

As the discourse at the Lusaka Chamber of Commerce progressed, the conversation turned towards the critical role of international aid and development assistance in promoting human development goals in the era of globalization.

Dr. Olivia, Marcus, Sofia, and their esteemed colleagues reconvened, their minds brimming with the complexities of this vital subpoint.

Dr. Olivia, her voice resonating with scholarly authority, addressed the assembled group once more. "International aid and development assistance play a crucial role in addressing global inequalities, fostering sustainable development, and advancing human welfare," she declared. "Yet, they also face challenges such as ineffective governance, dependency on donor funding, and the perpetuation of power imbalances."

Marcus, his gaze fixed on the horizon of global progress, stepped forward to share his reflections. "For countries grappling with poverty, conflict, and inequality, international aid offers a lifeline, providing vital resources, expertise, and support to build resilient and inclusive societies," he proclaimed. "However, it must be delivered in a way that respects local priorities, empowers communities, and promotes self-reliance for long-term sustainability."

Sofia, her empathy for the marginalized guiding her words, added her voice to the dialogue. "International aid has the potential to transform lives, lift people out of poverty, and build a more equitable world," she emphasized. "But it must be accountable, transparent, and driven by the principles of solidarity, cooperation, and respect for human rights."

As the discourse unfolded, a tapestry of perspectives emerged, weaving together the intricate dynamics of international aid and development assistance—illuminating both its promise and its challenges in the pursuit of global human welfare.

In the days and weeks that followed, Dr. Olivia, Marcus, Sofia, and their colleagues delved deeper into the complexities of international aid, exploring strategies to maximize its impact while addressing its limitations.

They engaged with policymakers, conducted research on best practices, and collaborated with development agencies and local communities to advocate for aid that was responsive to local needs, context-sensitive, and aligned with human development goals.

Their efforts sparked a renewed sense of solidarity and cooperation, inspiring individuals and communities to come together to harness the potential of international aid for shared prosperity and well-being.

And as the impact of globalization continued to unfold, a new vision emerged—one where international aid was not just a transactional exchange of resources, but a transformative force for human development, dignity, and solidarity across borders.

Global Governance: Ensuring Equity and Sustainability in a Connected World

As the dialogue unfolded at the Lusaka Chamber of Commerce, the spotlight shifted towards the imperative of global governance in ensuring equity and sustainability in an increasingly interconnected world.

Dr. Olivia, Marcus, Sofia, and their esteemed colleagues reconvened, their minds ignited with the complexities of this critical subpoint.

Dr. Olivia, her voice infused with scholarly wisdom, addressed the assembled group once more. "Global governance structures are essential for addressing transnational challenges, coordinating collective action, and promoting sustainable and equitable development," she declared. "Yet, they also face challenges such as power imbalances, lack of accountability, and resistance to reform."

Marcus, his entrepreneurial spirit undimmed, stepped forward to share his perspective. "For businesses operating in a globalized world, effective global governance provides a level playing field, reduces regulatory uncertainty, and fosters trust and stability," he proclaimed. "However, it also requires collaboration, transparency, and dialogue between governments, businesses, and civil society to ensure that governance frameworks prioritize people and planet over profit."

Sofia, her heart attuned to social justice, added her voice to the discourse. "Global governance is essential for addressing systemic inequalities, protecting human rights, and advancing environmental sustainability," she emphasized. "But it must be inclusive, participatory, and responsive to the needs and aspirations of all people, especially the most marginalized and vulnerable."

As the conversation unfolded, a tapestry of perspectives emerged, weaving together the intricate dynamics of global governance—illuminating both its potential as a force for positive change and the challenges inherent in its implementation.

In the days and weeks that followed, Dr. Olivia, Marcus, Sofia, and their colleagues delved deeper into the complexities of global governance, exploring strategies to strengthen accountability, enhance transparency, and promote democratic decision-making at the global level.

They engaged with policymakers, conducted research on governance mechanisms, and collaborated with international organizations and advocacy groups to advocate for reforms that prioritized equity, sustainability, and justice in global decision-making processes.

Their efforts sparked a renewed sense of urgency and purpose, inspiring individuals and communities to come together to demand more effective, inclusive, and equitable global governance structures.

And as the impact of globalization continued to unfold, a new vision emerged—one where global governance was not just a bureaucratic exercise, but a transformative force for building a more just, sustainable, and humane world for all.

Chapter Seven: The Future Trends of Work and Automation

In the hushed halls of the Lusaka Chamber of Commerce, a palpable sense of anticipation hung in the air as Dr. Olivia, Marcus, Sofia, and their esteemed colleagues gathered to explore the future trends of work and automation—a topic poised to redefine the very fabric of society.

Dr. Olivia, her voice steady with scholarly gravitas, addressed the assembled group. "The future of work stands at a crossroads, poised on the brink of transformative change driven by rapid technological advancements," she declared. "Automation, artificial intelligence, and robotics promise unprecedented efficiencies and opportunities, but they also raise profound questions about employment, inequality, and the nature of human labor."

Marcus, his eyes alight with entrepreneurial curiosity, stepped forward to share his perspective. "For businesses, automation represents a paradigm shift—a revolution in productivity, innovation, and competitiveness," he proclaimed. "Yet, it also demands adaptation, reskilling, and re-imagining of business models to navigate the complexities of a digitally driven economy."

Sofia, her empathy for the marginalized guiding her words, added her voice to the discourse. "The rise of automation threatens to exacerbate inequalities, displace workers, and deepen social divisions," she emphasized. "But it also presents opportunities for redefining work, fostering creativity, and addressing societal challenges in new and innovative ways."

As the conversation unfolded, a tapestry of perspectives emerged, weaving together the intricate dynamics of work and automation—illuminating both the promises of progress and the perils of disruption in the workforce of tomorrow.

In the days and weeks that followed, Dr. Olivia, Marcus, Sofia, and their colleagues delved deeper into the future trends of work, exploring strategies to navigate the challenges and harness the opportunities presented by automation.

They engaged with policymakers, conducted research on emerging technologies, and collaborated with industry leaders and labor organizations to advocate for policies that promote inclusive growth, lifelong learning, and social protection in the face of technological change.

Their efforts sparked a renewed sense of urgency and purpose, inspiring individuals and communities to come together to shape a future where the benefits of automation were equitably shared, and the dignity and well-being of all workers were safeguarded.

And as the impact of automation continued to unfold, a new vision emerged—one where human creativity, empathy, and ingenuity were valued as much as technological prowess, and where the future of work was not just about efficiency, but about meaningful contribution and fulfillment for all.

Technological Advances and Their Impact on Employment

As the conversation at the Lusaka Chamber of Commerce delved deeper into the future trends of work and automation, the focus shifted towards the profound impact of technological advances on employment—an aspect that held both promise and uncertainty for the workforce of tomorrow.

Dr. Olivia, Marcus, Sofia, and their esteemed colleagues reconvened, their minds ablaze with the complexities of this pivotal subpoint.

Dr. Olivia, her voice laced with scholarly insight, addressed the assembled group once more. "Technological advances have the potential to revolutionize industries, streamline processes, and create new opportunities for economic growth," she declared. "Yet, they also pose challenges such as job displacement, skills mismatches, and the erosion of traditional employment structures."

Marcus, his entrepreneurial spirit undimmed, stepped forward to share his insights. "For businesses, technological advances offer unprecedented efficiencies, allowing for greater productivity, innovation, and competitiveness," he proclaimed. "However, they also necessitate adaptation, reskilling, and investment in human capital to ensure that workers can thrive in a rapidly evolving digital landscape."

Sofia, her empathy for the workforce guiding her words, added her voice to the dialogue. "Technological advances have the potential to widen inequalities, exacerbate social divisions, and leave vulnerable workers behind," she emphasized. "But they also present opportunities for creativity, entrepreneurship, and the creation of new forms of work that prioritize

CHAPTER SEVEN: THE FUTURE TRENDS OF WORK AND AUTOMATION

human well-being and fulfillment."

As the discourse unfolded, a tapestry of perspectives emerged, weaving together the intricate dynamics of technological advances and their impact on employment—illuminating both the promises of progress and the challenges of adaptation in the face of rapid change.

In the days and weeks that followed, Dr. Olivia, Marcus, Sofia, and their colleagues delved deeper into the implications of technological advances, exploring strategies to mitigate the risks and maximize the benefits for workers and society as a whole.

They engaged with policymakers, conducted research on emerging technologies, and collaborated with industry stakeholders and labor unions to advocate for policies that fostered inclusive growth, lifelong learning, and social protection in the digital age.

Their efforts sparked a renewed sense of urgency and purpose, inspiring individuals and communities to come together to shape a future where technological advances served the common good, leaving no one behind.

And as the impact of technological advances continued to unfold, a new vision emerged—one where innovation was harnessed not just for profit, but for the betterment of humanity, and where the future of work was not just about automation, but about empowerment, dignity, and fulfillment for all.

Skills for the Future: Adapting to a Changing Labor Market

As the discussion at the Lusaka Chamber of Commerce unfolded, the spotlight shifted towards the crucial subpoint of skills for the future, highlighting the necessity of adapting to a changing labor market in the face of technological disruption.

Dr. Olivia, Marcus, Sofia, and their esteemed colleagues reconvened, their minds brimming with anticipation for the insights to come.

Dr. Olivia, her voice infused with scholarly wisdom, addressed the assembled group once more. "In the rapidly evolving landscape of work, the acquisition of new skills is paramount to ensuring individual resilience and collective prosperity," she declared. "Yet, the pace of technological change demands continuous learning, adaptability, and a reimagining of traditional education paradigms."

Marcus, his entrepreneurial spirit ignited by the prospect of innovation, stepped forward to share his perspective. "For workers, acquiring new skills opens doors to new opportunities, empowers them to stay relevant in the job market, and fosters a culture of lifelong learning," he proclaimed. "However, it also requires investment in training, upskilling, and access to quality education to bridge the gap between existing skills and emerging demands."

Sofia, her heart aligned with social justice, added her voice to the discourse. "The skills for the future must not only encompass technical competencies but also include critical thinking, creativity, emotional intelligence, and adaptability," she emphasized. "But they must also be accessible to all, regardless of background, socioeconomic status, or geographical location, to ensure that no one is left behind in the transition to a digital economy."

As the conversation unfolded, a tapestry of perspectives emerged, weaving together the intricate dynamics of skills for the future—illuminating both the potential for individual empowerment and the imperative for systemic transformation in education and training.

In the days and weeks that followed, Dr. Olivia, Marcus, Sofia, and their colleagues delved deeper into the implications of skills development, exploring strategies to foster a culture of lifelong learning, promote digital literacy, and enhance workforce readiness for the challenges of tomorrow.

They engaged with educators, policymakers, and industry leaders, conducted research on emerging skill sets, and collaborated with community organizations to advocate for inclusive and accessible education and training programs that empowered individuals to thrive in a rapidly changing world.

Their efforts sparked a renewed sense of purpose and possibility, inspiring individuals and communities to embrace the opportunities of lifelong learning and skill development as pathways to personal fulfillment, economic resilience, and social mobility.

And as the impact of technological disruption continued to unfold, a new vision emerged—one where skills for the future were not just a means of adaptation, but a catalyst for human potential and collective progress, leaving no one behind.

Universal Basic Income: A Potential Solution to Technological Unemployment

In the halls of the Lusaka Chamber of Commerce, the conversation shifted towards a provocative subpoint: Universal Basic Income (UBI) as a potential solution to technological unemployment—a topic that sparked both curiosity and controversy among the gathered minds.

Dr. Olivia, Marcus, Sofia, and their esteemed colleagues reconvened, their thoughts brimming with anticipation for the debate ahead.

Dr. Olivia, her voice tempered with academic rigor, addressed the assembled group once more. "As technological advancements reshape the labor market, the concept of Universal Basic Income has gained traction as a means of addressing the potential for widespread job displacement," she declared. "Yet, its implementation raises complex questions about sustainability, equity, and the future of work."

Marcus, his entrepreneurial spirit ignited by the prospect of innovation, stepped forward to share his perspective. "Universal Basic Income has the potential to provide a safety net for workers displaced by automation, enabling them to meet their basic needs and pursue retraining or entrepreneurial endeavors without the fear of financial ruin," he proclaimed. "However, it also requires careful consideration of funding mechanisms, incentives for workforce participation, and its impact on societal norms and values."

Sofia, her heart aligned with social justice, added her voice to the discourse. "Universal Basic Income has the potential to reduce poverty, alleviate inequality, and promote economic security for all," she emphasized. "But it must also be accompanied by complementary policies such as investment in education, healthcare, and social services to address the root causes of economic insecurity and promote social mobility."

As the conversation unfolded, a tapestry of perspectives emerged, weaving together the intricate dynamics of Universal Basic Income—illuminating both its promise as a tool for social justice and its challenges as a transformative policy intervention.

In the days and weeks that followed, Dr. Olivia, Marcus, Sofia, and their colleagues delved deeper into the implications of Universal Basic Income, exploring its feasibility, desirability, and potential impacts on society and the economy.

They engaged with policymakers, conducted research on pilot programs and case studies, and collaborated with advocacy groups to advocate for evidence-based policies that promoted economic security, dignity, and opportunity for all.

Their efforts sparked a renewed sense of debate and dialogue, inspiring individuals and communities to consider the possibilities of Universal Basic Income as a means of addressing the uncertainties of technological unemployment in the digital age.

And as the impact of automation continued to unfold, a new vision emerged—one where Universal Basic Income was not just a safety net, but a springboard for human potential and social progress, leaving no one behind.

Work-Life Balance: Rethinking Productivity and Well-Being

As the discussion at the Lusaka Chamber of Commerce continued, the focus shifted towards the crucial subpoint of work-life balance, prompting reflections on the intersection of productivity and well-being in the evolving landscape of work.

Dr. Olivia, Marcus, Sofia, and their esteemed colleagues reconvened, their minds buzzing with anticipation for the insights to come.

Dr. Olivia, her voice resonating with scholarly insight, addressed the assembled group once more. "In the pursuit of economic prosperity, the importance of work-life balance cannot be overstated," she declared. "As technological advancements reshape the nature of work, it becomes increasingly vital to prioritize the well-being of workers, fostering environments that promote both productivity and fulfillment."

Marcus, his entrepreneurial spirit undimmed, stepped forward to share his perspective. "For businesses, embracing work-life balance is not just a moral imperative but a strategic advantage," he proclaimed. "By prioritizing the health and happiness of employees, organizations can cultivate loyalty, creativity, and resilience, driving innovation and sustainable growth."

Sofia, her empathy for the workforce guiding her words, added her voice to the discourse. "Work-life balance is essential for fostering healthy, thriving communities," she emphasized. "It allows individuals to pursue their passions, cultivate relationships, and contribute meaningfully to society, leading to greater overall well-being and fulfillment."

CHAPTER SEVEN: THE FUTURE TRENDS OF WORK AND AUTOMATION

As the conversation unfolded, a tapestry of perspectives emerged, weaving together the intricate dynamics of work-life balance—illuminating both its importance as a cornerstone of human flourishing and its potential as a catalyst for organizational success.

In the days and weeks that followed, Dr. Olivia, Marcus, Sofia, and their colleagues delved deeper into the implications of work-life balance, exploring strategies to promote flexibility, autonomy, and mindfulness in the workplace.

They engaged with employers, conducted research on best practices, and collaborated with advocacy groups to advocate for policies that supported work-life integration, parental leave, and mental health support in the modern workforce.

Their efforts sparked a renewed sense of awareness and action, inspiring individuals and organizations to prioritize work-life balance as a fundamental aspect of a healthy, thriving society.

And as the impact of technological disruption continued to unfold, a new vision emerged—one where work was not just a means of production but a source of fulfillment, connection, and purpose, leaving no one behind.

The Gig Economy: Opportunities and Challenges for Workers

As the conversation at the Lusaka Chamber of Commerce delved deeper into the future of work, the spotlight shifted towards the complex subpoint of the gig economy—an aspect of modern employment that promised both opportunities and challenges for workers navigating the shifting landscape of work.

Dr. Olivia, Marcus, Sofia, and their esteemed colleagues reconvened, their minds buzzing with anticipation for the discussion ahead.

Dr. Olivia, her voice echoing with scholarly insight, addressed the assembled group once more. "The emergence of the gig economy has transformed the nature of work, offering flexibility, autonomy, and opportunities for entrepreneurship," she declared. "Yet, it also raises questions about job security, income stability, and the rights and protections of workers in an increasingly decentralized labor market."

Marcus, his entrepreneurial spirit ignited by the prospect of innovation, stepped forward to share his perspective. "For workers, the gig economy offers unprecedented freedom and flexibility, enabling them to pursue multiple income streams, balance work and life, and adapt to changing economic realities," he proclaimed. "However, it also poses challenges such as income volatility, lack of benefits, and limited access to social protections, raising concerns about the long-term sustainability of this model."

Sofia, her empathy for the workforce guiding her words, added her voice to the discourse. "The gig economy has the potential to democratize access to work, empower marginalized communities, and create opportunities for economic inclusion," she emphasized. "But it also requires safeguards to protect workers' rights, ensure fair wages, and address the growing precarity and inequality in the labor market."

As the conversation unfolded, a tapestry of perspectives emerged, weaving together the intricate dynamics of the gig economy—illuminating both its promises of flexibility and autonomy and its challenges of insecurity and exploitation for workers.

In the days and weeks that followed, Dr. Olivia, Marcus, Sofia, and their colleagues delved deeper into the implications of the gig economy, exploring strategies to maximize its benefits while mitigating its risks for workers and society as a whole.

They engaged with policymakers, conducted research on labor regulations, and collaborated with gig workers and advocacy groups to advocate for policies that ensured fair wages, access to benefits, and protections for gig workers in the digital age.

Their efforts sparked a renewed sense of urgency and advocacy, inspiring individuals and communities to come together to shape a future where the gig economy served as a source of opportunity and empowerment for all workers.

And as the impact of technological disruption continued to unfold, a new vision emerged—one where the gig economy was not just a side hustle but a viable pathway to economic independence and fulfillment, leaving no one behind.

Policy Responses to Automation: Ensuring Inclusive Economic Growth

As the dialogue at the Lusaka Chamber of Commerce progressed, attention turned towards a critical subpoint: policy responses to automation—an aspect that demanded careful consideration to ensure inclusive economic growth in the face of technological disruption.

Dr. Olivia, Marcus, Sofia, and their esteemed colleagues gathered once more, their minds ablaze with anticipation for the discourse ahead.

Dr. Olivia, her voice resonating with scholarly insight, addressed the assembled group. "Policy responses to automation are crucial for shaping the future of work and ensuring that the benefits of technological advancement are shared equitably among all members of society," she declared. "Yet, they must strike a delicate balance between promoting innovation and protecting workers' rights and livelihoods."

Marcus, his entrepreneurial spirit undimmed, stepped forward to share his perspective. "For policymakers, responding to automation requires foresight, adaptability, and a willingness to experiment with new approaches," he proclaimed. "They must invest in education and training, support displaced workers, and create incentives for businesses to adopt responsible automation practices that prioritize job quality and worker well-being."

Sofia, her heart aligned with social justice, added her voice to the discourse. "Policy responses to automation must be rooted in principles of equity, justice, and inclusivity," she emphasized. "They must address the structural inequalities exacerbated by technological change, ensure that vulnerable communities are not left behind, and foster an economy that works for all, not just the few."

As the conversation unfolded, a tapestry of perspectives emerged, weaving together the intricate dynamics of policy responses to automation—illuminating both the opportunities for progress and the challenges of implementation in a rapidly changing world.

In the days and weeks that followed, Dr. Olivia, Marcus, Sofia, and their colleagues delved deeper into the implications of policy responses to automation, exploring strategies to promote inclusive economic growth, mitigate the risks of job displacement, and build resilient communities in the face of technological disruption.

They engaged with policymakers, conducted research on best practices, and collaborated with advocacy groups to advocate for policies that prioritized workers' rights, invested in human capital, and fostered an economy that worked for the benefit of all members of society.

Their efforts sparked a renewed sense of purpose and possibility, inspiring individuals and communities to come together to shape a future where automation served as a tool for human progress and prosperity, leaving no one behind.

8

Chapter Eight: Behavioral Insights for Policy Making

In the corridors of power, where decisions that shape the fate of nations are made, a new chapter unfolds—a chapter that delves into the realm of behavioral insights for policy making, where the complexities of human behavior meet the imperatives of governance.

In the hallowed halls of the National Policy Institute, Dr. Olivia, Marcus, Sofia, and their esteemed colleagues gathered, their minds poised to explore the intersection of psychology, economics, and public policy.

Dr. Olivia, her voice resolute with scholarly authority, addressed the assembly. "Behavioral insights offer a powerful lens through which policymakers can understand and influence the decisions of individuals and societies," she declared. "By tapping into the quirks and biases of human behavior, we can design more effective policies that promote better outcomes for all."

Marcus, his entrepreneurial zeal ignited by the prospect of innovation, stepped forward to share his perspective. "For policymakers, behavioral insights provide a roadmap for crafting policies that nudge people towards positive behaviors, whether it's saving for retirement, adopting healthier lifestyles, or contributing to the common good," he proclaimed. "By leveraging the principles of behavioral economics, we can design interventions that are not only more effective but also more humane and empathetic."

Sofia, her commitment to social justice guiding her words, added her voice to the discourse. "Behavioral insights have the potential to address some of the most pressing challenges facing society, from poverty and inequality to environmental degradation and public health," she emphasized. "But they must also be wielded responsibly, with careful consideration for ethics, equity, and the dignity of individuals."

As the conversation unfolded, a tapestry of perspectives emerged, weaving together the intricate dynamics of behavioral insights for policy making—illuminating both the promise of progress and the imperative for ethical governance in harnessing the power of human behavior.

In the days and weeks that followed, Dr. Olivia, Marcus, Sofia, and their colleagues delved deeper into the implications of behavioral insights, exploring strategies to integrate behavioral science into the policy making process, foster interdisciplinary collaboration, and promote evidence-based decision-making at all levels of government.

They engaged with policymakers, conducted research on behavioral interventions, and collaborated with behavioral scientists and practitioners to advocate for policies that were informed by a nuanced understanding of human behavior and psychology.

Their efforts sparked a renewed sense of curiosity and

commitment, inspiring policymakers to embrace behavioral insights as a tool for transformative change, and empowering individuals and communities to make better choices for themselves and society as a whole.

And as the impact of behavioral insights continued to unfold, a new vision emerged—one where policy making was not just a matter of ideology or partisan politics but a science informed by the complexities of human behavior, leaving no one behind.

Nudging for Good: Using Behavioral Science to Shape Public Policy

As the discussion at the National Policy Institute continued, the focus shifted towards a pivotal subpoint: nudging for good—an exploration of how behavioral science could be leveraged to shape public policy for the betterment of society.

Dr. Olivia, Marcus, Sofia, and their esteemed colleagues reconvened, their minds alight with the possibilities ahead.

Dr. Olivia, her voice infused with scholarly wisdom, addressed the assembly. "Nudging for good entails the strategic use of behavioral insights to encourage positive behaviors and improve societal outcomes," she declared. "By designing choice architectures that make desirable behaviors more accessible and attractive, policymakers can steer individuals towards decisions that benefit both themselves and the greater good."

Marcus, his entrepreneurial spirit ignited by the prospect of innovation, stepped forward to share his perspective. "For policymakers, nudging for good represents a paradigm shift in how we approach governance," he proclaimed. "Rather than relying solely on regulation or incentives, we can subtly influence behavior through simple, cost-effective interventions that preserve individual autonomy while fostering collective well-being."

Sofia, her commitment to social justice guiding her words, added her voice to the discourse. "Nudging for good must be guided by principles of transparency, accountability, and respect for human dignity," she emphasized. "It should empower individuals to make informed choices that align with their values and aspirations, rather than manipulating or coercing them into compliance."

As the conversation unfolded, a tapestry of perspectives emerged, weaving together the intricate dynamics of nudging for good—illuminating both its potential for positive change and the ethical considerations that must accompany its implementation.

In the days and weeks that followed, Dr. Olivia, Marcus, Sofia, and their colleagues delved deeper into the implications of nudging for good, exploring strategies to apply behavioral science principles in diverse policy domains, from public health and environmental conservation to financial literacy and civic engagement.

They engaged with policymakers, conducted research on behavioral interventions, and collaborated with community stakeholders to design and implement nudges that promoted social good and fostered a culture of responsible citizenship.

Their efforts sparked a renewed sense of optimism and innovation, inspiring policymakers to embrace nudging as a tool for solving complex societal challenges and empowering individuals to make positive choices for themselves and their communities.

And as the impact of nudging for good continued to unfold,

a new vision emerged—one where public policy was not just a top-down imposition but a collaborative effort that harnessed the insights of behavioral science to create a more just, equitable, and compassionate society, leaving no one behind.

Behavioral Insights for Policy Making

Within the hallowed halls of the National Policy Institute, the discourse delved deeper into the realm of behavioral insights, focusing now on the critical subpoint of behavioral public finance—a domain where the principles of human behavior intersect with the complexities of fiscal policy to promote responsible financial behavior among citizens.

Dr. Olivia, Marcus, Sofia, and their esteemed colleagues reconvened, their minds ablaze with the potential for positive change.

Dr. Olivia, her voice resolute with scholarly authority, addressed the assembly once more. "Behavioral public finance offers a revolutionary approach to fiscal policy, one that recognizes the irrationality and biases inherent in human decision-making," she declared. "By leveraging these insights, policymakers can design interventions that promote savings, reduce debt, and foster long-term financial security for individuals and families."

Marcus, his entrepreneurial spirit undimmed, stepped forward to share his perspective. "For policymakers, behavioral public finance represents an opportunity to address the root causes of financial instability and inequality," he proclaimed. "By nudging citizens towards prudent financial decisions through targeted interventions such as default options, commitment devices, and personalized feedback, we can empower individuals to take control of their financial futures."

Sofia, her commitment to social justice guiding her words, added her voice to the discourse. "Behavioral public finance must prioritize the needs of vulnerable populations and promote equitable access to financial resources," she emphasized. "It should address systemic barriers to financial inclusion and empower marginalized communities to build assets, accumulate wealth, and achieve economic independence."

As the conversation unfolded, a tapestry of perspectives emerged, weaving together the intricate dynamics of behavioral public finance—illuminating both its potential to transform financial behavior and its imperative to promote social justice and equity.

In the days and weeks that followed, Dr. Olivia, Marcus, Sofia, and their colleagues delved deeper into the implications of behavioral public finance, exploring strategies to apply behavioral insights in diverse policy domains, from retirement savings and consumer credit to taxation and social welfare.

They engaged with policymakers, conducted research on behavioral interventions, and collaborated with financial institutions and community organizations to design and implement initiatives that promoted responsible financial behavior and economic empowerment for all.

Their efforts sparked a renewed sense of hope and empowerment, inspiring individuals and communities to take control of their financial destinies and build a more resilient and inclusive economy for future generations.

And as the impact of behavioral public finance continued to unfold, a new vision emerged—one where fiscal policy was not just about balancing budgets or maximizing revenue but about empowering citizens to achieve financial well-being and pursue their dreams, leaving no one behind.

Health Policy and Behavioral Economics: Encouraging Healthy Choices

As the discussion at the National Policy Institute progressed, the spotlight shifted towards a pivotal subpoint: health policy and behavioral economics—a domain where the principles of human behavior intersect with the imperatives of public health to encourage healthy choices among citizens.

Dr. Olivia, Marcus, Sofia, and their esteemed colleagues reconvened, their minds ablaze with the potential to improve public well-being.

Dr. Olivia, her voice infused with scholarly insight, addressed the assembly once more. "Health policy and behavioral economics offer a powerful framework for promoting preventive care, reducing risky behaviors, and improving overall health outcomes," she declared. "By understanding the cognitive biases and social influences that shape health-related decisions, policymakers can design interventions that nudge individuals towards healthier choices and lifestyles."

Marcus, his entrepreneurial spirit ignited by the prospect of innovation, stepped forward to share his perspective. "For policymakers, health policy and behavioral economics represent an opportunity to tackle some of the most pressing health challenges of our time," he proclaimed. "By leveraging insights from behavioral science, we can design interventions that make healthy options more accessible, attractive, and convenient, empowering individuals to take control of their health and well-being."

Sofia, her commitment to social justice guiding her words, added her voice to the discourse. "Health policy and behavioral economics must prioritize equity and address the social determinants of health," she emphasized. "It should aim to reduce health disparities, improve access to care, and promote health equity for all individuals and communities, regardless of their socio-economic status or background."

As the conversation unfolded, a tapestry of perspectives emerged, weaving together the intricate dynamics of health policy and behavioral economics—illuminating both its potential to revolutionize public health and its imperative to address systemic inequalities and injustices.

In the days and weeks that followed, Dr. Olivia, Marcus, Sofia, and their colleagues delved deeper into the implications of health policy and behavioral economics, exploring strategies to apply behavioral insights in diverse policy domains, from smoking cessation and healthy eating to vaccination and chronic disease management.

They engaged with policymakers, conducted research on behavioral interventions, and collaborated with healthcare providers and community organizations to design and implement initiatives that promoted healthy behaviors and improved health outcomes for all.

Their efforts sparked a renewed sense of optimism and empowerment, inspiring individuals and communities to take charge of their health and well-being, and advocating for policies that prioritized prevention, early intervention, and health equity.

And as the impact of health policy and behavioral economics continued to unfold, a new vision emerged—one where health was not just the absence of disease but a state of holistic well-being, where every individual had the opportunity to live a healthy, fulfilling life, leaving no one behind.

Environmental Policy and Behavioral Insights: Promoting Sustainable Behavior

Within the grand chambers of the National Policy Institute, the discourse deepened, turning now to a crucial subpoint: environmental policy and behavioral insights—a realm where the intricacies of human behavior converge with the imperative of ecological stewardship to promote sustainable behaviors among citizens.

Dr. Olivia, Marcus, Sofia, and their esteemed colleagues reconvened, their minds aflame with the possibilities of fostering a greener, more sustainable future.

Dr. Olivia, her voice resounding with scholarly authority, addressed the assembly once more. "Environmental policy and behavioral insights offer a transformative approach to addressing the urgent challenges of climate change, pollution, and resource depletion," she declared. "By understanding the psychological drivers and social dynamics that influence environmental behaviors, policymakers can design interventions that nudge individuals and communities towards more sustainable choices and lifestyles."

Marcus, his entrepreneurial spirit ignited by the prospect of innovation, stepped forward to share his perspective. "For policymakers, environmental policy and behavioral insights represent an opportunity to harness the power of human behavior for the greater good of the planet," he proclaimed. "By leveraging insights from behavioral science, we can design interventions that make sustainable options more appealing, convenient, and socially normative, empowering individuals to adopt Eco-friendly behaviors and reduce their environmental footprint."

Sofia, her commitment to social justice guiding her words, added her voice to the discourse. "Environmental policy and behavioral insights must prioritize equity and environmental justice," she emphasized. "It should aim to address the disproportionate impacts of environmental degradation on marginalized communities, empower grassroots movements, and promote inclusive, community-driven solutions that advance both sustainability and social equity."

As the conversation unfolded, a tapestry of perspectives emerged, weaving together the intricate dynamics of environmental policy and behavioral insights—illuminating both its potential to catalyze transformative change and its imperative to center equity and justice in sustainability efforts.

In the days and weeks that followed, Dr. Olivia, Marcus, Sofia, and their colleagues delved deeper into the implications of environmental policy and behavioral insights, exploring strategies to apply behavioral interventions in diverse policy domains, from energy conservation and waste reduction to sustainable transportation and conservation efforts.

They engaged with policymakers, conducted research on behavioral interventions, and collaborated with environmental organizations and community groups to design and implement initiatives that promoted sustainable behaviors and fostered a culture of environmental stewardship among citizens.

Their efforts sparked a renewed sense of urgency and solidarity, inspiring individuals and communities to take collective action to protect the planet and secure a sustainable future for generations to come.

And as the impact of environmental policy and behavioral insights continued to unfold, a new vision emerged—one where environmental sustainability was not just a lofty goal but a shared responsibility and a collective endeavor, leaving no one behind.

Education Policy: Applying Behavioral Science to Improve Learning Outcomes

In the echoing halls of the National Policy Institute, the discourse shifted once more, now focusing on a pivotal subpoint: education policy and its intersection with behavioral science—a realm where the complexities of human behavior converge with the imperative of fostering optimal learning outcomes among students.

Dr. Olivia, Marcus, Sofia, and their esteemed colleagues reconvened, their minds brimming with the potential to revolutionize education through the lens of behavioral insights.

Dr. Olivia, her voice resonant with scholarly wisdom, addressed the assembly once more. "Education policy and behavioral science offer a transformative approach to addressing the challenges of student engagement, academic achievement, and educational equity," she declared. "By understanding the cognitive biases, motivational factors, and social dynamics that influence learning behaviors, policymakers can design interventions that enhance learning experiences and improve outcomes for all students."

Marcus, his entrepreneurial spirit ignited by the prospect of innovation, stepped forward to share his perspective. "For policymakers, education policy and behavioral insights represent an opportunity to re-imagine the educational landscape and unlock the full potential of every student," he proclaimed. "By leveraging insights from behavioral science, we can design interventions that promote intrinsic motivation, foster a growth mindset, and create environments that support optimal learning and development."

Sofia, her commitment to social justice guiding her words, added her voice to the discourse. "Education policy and behavioral insights must prioritize equity and inclusivity," she emphasized. "It should aim to address the systemic barriers to educational access and success faced by marginalized communities, promote culturally responsive teaching practices, and create pathways for all students to thrive, regardless of their background or circumstances."

As the conversation unfolded, a tapestry of perspectives emerged, weaving together the intricate dynamics of education policy and behavioral insights—illuminating both its potential to transform education and its imperative to address systemic inequalities and injustices.

In the days and weeks that followed, Dr. Olivia, Marcus, Sofia, and their colleagues delved deeper into the implications of education policy and behavioral insights, exploring strategies to apply behavioral interventions in diverse educational settings, from early childhood education and K-12 schooling to higher education and lifelong learning.

They engaged with policymakers, conducted research on effective teaching practices, and collaborated with educators, parents, and students to design and implement initiatives that promoted student engagement, academic achievement, and social-emotional development.

Their efforts sparked a renewed sense of hope and empowerment, inspiring educators to embrace innovative teaching methods, students to take ownership of their learning, and communities to come together to support educational excellence for all.

And as the impact of education policy and behavioral insights continued to unfold, a new vision emerged—one where education was not just a means to an end but a transformative journey that empowered individuals to reach their fullest potential, leaving no one behind.

Ethical Considerations in Policy Design: Balancing Effectiveness with Respect for Human Dignity

Within the prestigious halls of the National Policy Institute, the discourse evolved, now delving into a pivotal subpoint: ethical considerations in policy design—a domain where the principles of behavioral science intersect with the imperative of upholding human dignity and rights in governance.

Dr. Olivia, Marcus, Sofia, and their esteemed colleagues reconvened, their minds stirred by the profound ethical implications of their work.

Dr. Olivia, her voice imbued with scholarly integrity, addressed the assembly once more. "Ethical considerations in policy design are paramount, as they guide us in navigating the delicate balance between effectiveness and the preservation of human dignity," she declared. "By upholding ethical principles such as autonomy, beneficence, non-maleficence, and justice, policymakers can ensure that their interventions respect the rights and values of individuals and communities."

Marcus, his entrepreneurial spirit tempered by a commitment to integrity, stepped forward to share his perspective.

"For policymakers, ethical considerations are not just a matter of compliance, but a moral imperative," he proclaimed. "By aligning policies with ethical principles, we can ensure that our interventions promote the well-being and flourishing of all individuals, without sacrificing their fundamental rights or freedoms."

Sofia, her dedication to social justice guiding her words, added her voice to the discourse. "Ethical considerations in policy design must prioritize the needs and voices of marginalized communities," she emphasized. "It should aim to address systemic injustices, empower vulnerable populations, and foster a culture of respect, inclusion, and equity in governance."

As the conversation unfolded, a tapestry of perspectives emerged, weaving together the intricate dynamics of ethical considerations in policy design—illuminating both its importance in safeguarding human rights and its imperative in promoting social justice and equity.

In the days and weeks that followed, Dr. Olivia, Marcus, Sofia, and their colleagues grappled with the ethical dimensions of their work, engaging in thoughtful deliberation, ethical reflection, and consultation with stakeholders to ensure that their policies were grounded in principles of justice, fairness, and respect for human dignity.

Their efforts sparked a renewed commitment to ethical governance, inspiring policymakers to uphold the highest standards of integrity, transparency, and accountability in their decision-making processes.

And as the impact of ethical considerations in policy design continued to unfold, a new vision emerged—one where policies were not just effective, but also ethical, promoting the common good and protecting the rights and dignity of every individual, leaving no one behind.

9

Chapter Nine: Community Development and Empowerment

In the heart of Lusaka, amidst the bustling streets and towering Buildings, lies a neighborhood teeming with life, diversity, and untapped potential. It is here that the journey of community development and empowerment begins—a tale of resilience, solidarity, and the transformative power of collective action.

Dr. Olivia, Marcus, Sofia, and their fellow advocates gather under the shade of an old oak tree, their voices alive with determination and hope. They are joined by a diverse array of community members—residents, activists, small business owners, and neighborhood leaders—all united in their vision of a brighter future for their community.

Dr. Olivia, her eyes sparkling with passion, addresses the gathering. "Community development and empowerment are not just about building infrastructure or implementing programs," she declares. "They are about harnessing the collective wisdom, creativity, and resources of the community to create positive change from within."

Marcus, his voice resolute with conviction, steps forward to share his vision. "For too long, our community has been overlooked and underserved," he proclaims. "But today, we stand together as agents of change, ready to unlock the untapped potential of our neighborhood and create a future that reflects our hopes, dreams, and aspirations."

Sofia, her spirit ignited by the spirit of solidarity, adds her voice to the chorus. "Community development and empowerment must be rooted in principles of equity, inclusion, and justice," she emphasizes. "It should aim to address systemic barriers, amplify the voices of marginalized groups, and create opportunities for all members of the community to thrive and succeed."

As the conversation unfolds, a sense of unity and purpose pervades the gathering, weaving together the hopes, dreams, and aspirations of each individual into a shared vision for the future.

In the days and weeks that follow, Dr. Olivia, Marcus, Sofia, and their fellow advocates embark on a journey of community engagement, collaboration, and empowerment. They work side by side with community members to identify priorities, develop strategies, and implement initiatives that address the unique needs and challenges of their neighborhood.

Together, they revitalize parks and public spaces, support local businesses and entrepreneurs, organize cultural events and festivals, and create pathways for youth engagement and leadership development.

Their efforts spark a renewed sense of pride and belonging among residents, inspiring them to take ownership of their community and become active participants in its transformation.

And as the impact of community development and empowerment continues to unfold, a new chapter begins—a chapter where the power of community is unleashed, and the promise of a brighter future becomes a reality for all who call Lusaka home.

Community-Based Approaches to Economic Development

In the heart of Lusaka, amidst the vibrant community gathering, the focus shifts to a critical subpoint: community-based approaches to economic development—a realm where the collective aspirations of residents intersect with innovative strategies to stimulate local economies and create opportunities for prosperity.

Dr. Olivia, Marcus, Sofia, and their fellow advocates stand before the gathered crowd, their voices infused with a sense of purpose and possibility.

Dr. Olivia, her gaze sweeping across the diverse faces before her, begins to speak. "Community-based approaches to economic development recognize that the true engines of growth and innovation lie within the community itself," she declares. "By harnessing the unique assets, talents, and resources of our neighborhood, we can create a more resilient and equitable economy that benefits everyone."

Marcus, his entrepreneurial spirit ignited by the prospect of local empowerment, steps forward to share his vision. "For too long, our community has relied on outside investments and initiatives to drive economic growth," he proclaims. "But today, we stand poised to chart our own course—to support local businesses, foster entrepreneurship, and create pathways for economic opportunity that are rooted in our shared values and aspirations."

Sofia, her commitment to social justice guiding her words, adds her voice to the conversation. "Community-based approaches to economic development must prioritize equity and inclusion," she emphasizes. "They should aim to address the systemic barriers that have marginalized certain groups, empower residents to participate fully in the economy, and ensure that the benefits of growth are shared by all members of our community."

As the discussion unfolds, a sense of optimism and determination fills the air, as residents come together to envision a future where economic prosperity is not just a distant dream, but a tangible reality within reach.

In the days and weeks that follow, Dr. Olivia, Marcus, Sofia, and their fellow advocates roll up their sleeves and get to work, collaborating with local stakeholders to identify economic opportunities, leverage existing assets, and develop strategies for sustainable growth.

Together, they launch initiatives to support small businesses, provide access to capital and technical assistance, and create pathways for workforce development and job training.

Their efforts begin to bear fruit, as new businesses open their doors, residents find employment opportunities, and the local economy experiences a newfound vitality and resilience.

And as the impact of community-based approaches to economic development continues to unfold, a new narrative emerges—a narrative of empowerment, innovation, and possibility.

Participatory Development: Engaging Communities in Decision Making

In the heart of Lusaka, amidst the vibrant community gathering, the conversation shifts to a pivotal subpoint: participatory development—a concept that embodies the essence of empowerment by engaging communities in decision-making processes that shape their own future.

Dr. Olivia, Marcus, Sofia, and their fellow advocates stand before the eager crowd, their voices resonating with the spirit of collaboration and inclusion.

Dr. Olivia, her eyes sparkling with enthusiasm, addresses the gathered community members. "Participatory development is more than just a buzzword—it's a philosophy that recognizes the wisdom and expertise that resides within our community," she declares. "By involving residents in the decision-making process, we can ensure that our initiatives are responsive to local needs, values, and aspirations."

Marcus, his belief in the power of grassroots leadership unwavering, steps forward to share his perspective. "For too long, decisions about our community have been made by distant bureaucrats and politicians," he proclaims. "But today, we have the opportunity to reclaim our voice and shape our own destiny—to participate in the decisions that affect our lives and the lives of our neighbors."

Sofia, her commitment to social justice guiding her words, adds her voice to the chorus. "Participatory development must prioritize inclusivity and equity," she emphasizes. "It should aim to amplify the voices of marginalized groups, ensure that decision-making processes are transparent and accessible to all, and create pathways for meaningful participation that empower residents to become agents of change in their own communities."

As the discussion unfolds, a sense of excitement and possibility fills the air, as residents come together to envision a future where everyone has a seat at the table and a voice in shaping the direction of their community.

In the days and weeks that follow, Dr. Olivia, Marcus, Sofia, and their fellow advocates work tirelessly to turn the principles of participatory development into reality. They organize community forums and town hall meetings, establish neighborhood councils and advisory committees, and implement mechanisms for feedback and accountability.

Together, they create a culture of collaboration and co-creation, where residents are empowered to share their ideas, express their concerns, and contribute their talents to the collective good.

Their efforts begin to bear fruit, as residents become actively engaged in decision-making processes, providing input on everything from neighborhood revitalization projects to public policy initiatives.

And as the impact of participatory development continues to unfold, a new spirit of empowerment takes hold—a spirit that transcends individual interests and unites the community in a shared vision of progress and prosperity.

Asset-Based Community Development: Leveraging Local Resources for Growth

In the heart of Lusaka, amidst the bustling community gathering, the focus shifts to a crucial subpoint: asset-based community development—a concept that embodies the idea of leveraging local resources, talents, and strengths to foster growth and resilience from within.

Dr. Olivia, Marcus, Sofia, and their fellow advocates stand before the assembled residents, their voices imbued with a sense of optimism and possibility.

Dr. Olivia, her eyes alight with passion, addresses the crowd. "Asset-based community development recognizes that every community possesses unique strengths and resources that can be harnessed to drive positive change," she declares. "By identifying and leveraging these assets, we can create a foundation for sustainable growth and resilience that empowers residents to shape their own destiny."

Marcus, his belief in the power of entrepreneurship and innovation unwavering, steps forward to share his vision. "For too long, our community has been defined by its challenges and deficits," he proclaims. "But today, we have the opportunity to shift the narrative—to focus on our strengths and assets, and to build a future that reflects our collective potential."

Sofia, her commitment to social justice guiding her words, adds her voice to the conversation. "Asset-based community development must prioritize inclusivity and equity," she emphasizes. "It should aim to amplify the voices of marginalized groups, ensure that resources are distributed equitably, and create opportunities for all residents to participate in and benefit from the development process."

As the discussion unfolds, a sense of excitement and possibility fills the air, as residents come together to celebrate the richness and diversity of their community's assets.

In the days and weeks that follow, Dr. Olivia, Marcus, Sofia, and their fellow advocates work tirelessly to translate the principles of asset-based community development into action. They conduct asset mapping exercises, engage residents in asset-based planning processes, and facilitate partnerships between local organizations, businesses, and institutions.

Together, they uncover a wealth of untapped resources, from community gardens and cultural institutions to small businesses and grassroots organizations, each offering its own unique contribution to the community's well-being.

Their efforts begin to yield results, as residents discover new opportunities for collaboration, innovation, and growth. Community gardens flourish, local businesses thrive, and cultural events and festivals celebrate the diversity and vibrancy of the community.

And as the impact of asset-based community development continues to unfold, a new sense of pride and resilience takes hold—a spirit that transcends challenges and unites residents in a shared vision of hope and possibility.

Social Entrepreneurship: Harnessing Innovation for Social Good

In the heart of Lusaka, amidst the lively community gathering, attention shifts to a pivotal subpoint: social entrepreneurship—a concept that embodies the spirit of innovation, creativity, and altruism in addressing social challenges and driving positive change.

Dr. Olivia, Marcus, Sofia, and their fellow advocates stand before the engaged audience, their voices carrying the energy of possibility and transformation.

Dr. Olivia, her enthusiasm contagious, addresses the crowd. "Social entrepreneurship offers a powerful approach to community development, one that combines the innovative spirit of entrepreneurship with a commitment to social good," she declares. "By harnessing the creativity and passion of our residents, we can unlock new solutions to age-old problems and create lasting impact in our community."

Marcus, his entrepreneurial zeal ignited by the prospect of making a difference, steps forward to share his vision. "For too long, we've relied on traditional models of charity and philanthropy to address social issues," he proclaims. "But today, we have the opportunity to think differently—to leverage the power of entrepreneurship to create sustainable, scalable solutions that tackle root causes and empower individuals to build better lives for themselves and their communities."

Sofia, her commitment to social justice guiding her words, adds her voice to the conversation. "Social entrepreneurship must prioritize equity and inclusion," she emphasizes. "It should aim to address systemic injustices, amplify the voices of marginalized groups, and create opportunities for all residents to participate in and benefit from the entrepreneurial ecosystem."

As the discussion unfolds, a sense of possibility and excitement fills the air, as residents envision the potential for social entrepreneurship to drive meaningful change in their community.

In the days and weeks that follow, Dr. Olivia, Marcus, Sofia, and their fellow advocates work tirelessly to cultivate a culture of social entrepreneurship in Lusaka. They host workshops and training sessions, connect aspiring entrepreneurs with mentors and resources, and facilitate partnerships between local businesses, nonprofits, and government agencies.

Together, they inspire a new generation of change makers to pursue ventures that not only generate profits but also create positive social and environmental impact.

Their efforts begin to bear fruit, as social enterprises emerge to tackle a wide range of issues, from food insecurity and affordable housing to environmental sustainability and access to education. These ventures not only provide innovative solutions to pressing challenges but also create jobs, empower communities, and drive economic growth.

And as the impact of social entrepreneurship continues to unfold, a new spirit of possibility and resilience takes hold—a spirit that transcends boundaries and empowers residents to take ownership of their future.

CHAPTER NINE: COMMUNITY DEVELOPMENT AND EMPOWERMENT

Microfinance and Financial Inclusion: Empowering Communities Through Access to Capital

In the heart of Lusaka, amid the bustling community gathering, the conversation pivots to a pivotal subpoint: microfinance and financial inclusion—a concept that embodies the empowerment of communities through access to capital and financial resources.

Dr. Olivia, Marcus, Sofia, and their fellow advocates stand before the attentive audience, their voices resonating with determination and hope.

Dr. Olivia, her passion for economic justice evident, addresses the crowd. "Microfinance and financial inclusion are powerful tools for empowering communities and unlocking economic opportunities," she declares. "By providing access to capital and financial services, we can enable entrepreneurs to start or expand businesses, families to invest in education and healthcare, and individuals to build assets and secure their futures."

Marcus, his belief in the transformative power of entrepreneurship unwavering, steps forward to share his perspective. "For too long, financial exclusion has held back our community, preventing talented individuals from realizing their dreams and stifling economic growth," he proclaims. "But today, we have the opportunity to change that—to break down barriers and create pathways to prosperity for all."

Sofia, her commitment to social justice guiding her words, adds her voice to the conversation. "Microfinance and financial inclusion must prioritize equity and inclusion," she emphasizes. "They should aim to reach marginalized groups, empower women and minorities, and ensure that no one is left behind in the pursuit of economic opportunity."

As the discussion unfolds, a sense of possibility and empowerment fills the air, as residents imagine the impact that access to capital and financial services could have on their lives and their community.

In the days and weeks that follow, Dr. Olivia, Marcus, Sofia, and their fellow advocates work tirelessly to make financial inclusion a reality in Lusaka. They partner with local banks and credit unions to expand access to affordable banking services, launch microfinance programs to provide small loans to aspiring entrepreneurs, and offer financial literacy workshops to empower residents to make informed decisions about their finances.

Together, they break down barriers and create pathways to economic opportunity for all residents, regardless of their background or circumstances.

Their efforts begin to bear fruit, as individuals and families gain access to the capital they need to start businesses, buy homes, and invest in their futures. Entrepreneurs launch new ventures, create jobs, and stimulate economic growth, while families build assets, improve their living standards, and achieve financial security.

And as the impact of microfinance and financial inclusion continues to unfold, a new era of opportunity and prosperity dawns in Lusaka—a future where every resident has the tools and resources they need to thrive and succeed.

Place-Based Development Strategies: Tailoring Solutions to Local Contexts

In the heart of Lusaka, amidst the community gathering, the discussion shifts to a critical subpoint: place-based development strategies—a concept that recognizes the unique characteristics and challenges of each neighborhood, and tailors solutions to meet their specific needs.

Dr. Olivia, Marcus, Sofia, and their fellow advocates stand before the attentive audience, their voices resonating with empathy and determination.

Dr. Olivia, her eyes alight with passion, addresses the crowd. "Place-based development strategies offer a holistic approach to community empowerment," she declares. "By understanding the unique assets, strengths, and challenges of each neighborhood, we can tailor solutions that are responsive to local contexts and foster sustainable, equitable growth."

Marcus, his belief in the power of localized solutions unwavering, steps forward to share his perspective. "For too long, one-size-fits-all approaches have failed to address the diverse needs of our community," he proclaims. "But today, we have the opportunity to change that—to embrace the richness and complexity of our neighborhoods, and to co-create solutions that reflect the aspirations and priorities of our residents."

Sofia, her commitment to social justice guiding her words, adds her voice to the conversation. "Place-based development strategies must prioritize equity and inclusion," she emphasizes. "They should aim to engage residents as active participants in the decision-making process, amplify the voices of marginalized groups, and create opportunities for all members of the community to contribute to and benefit from local development initiatives."

As the discussion unfolds, a sense of possibility and empowerment fills the air, as residents imagine the impact that place-based development strategies could have on their neighborhoods and their lives.

In the days and weeks that follow, Dr. Olivia, Marcus, Sofia, and their fellow advocates work tirelessly to implement place-based development strategies in Lusaka. They conduct community assessments and stakeholder consultations to identify priorities and opportunities, develop neighborhood-specific action plans to address key challenges, and mobilize resources and support to bring these plans to fruition.

Together, they empower residents to take ownership of their neighborhoods, fostering a sense of pride, belonging, and agency that transcends individual projects and initiatives.

Their efforts begin to yield results, as neighborhoods across Lusaka experience a revitalization and renewal fueled by the creativity and energy of their residents. Community gardens spring up in vacant lots, neighborhood businesses thrive, and public spaces become vibrant hubs of activity and connection.

And as the impact of place-based development strategies continues to unfold, a new sense of hope and possibility takes hold—a spirit that transcends boundaries and empowers residents to shape their own destinies, one neighborhood at a time.

10

Chapter Ten: Human-Centered Financial Systems

In the heart of Lusaka, where the city skyline looms tall and the rhythm of life pulses through its streets, a gathering of minds convenes to explore the transformative potential of human-centered financial systems.

Dr. Olivia, Marcus, Sofia, and a diverse array of stakeholders stand before an audience eager for change, their voices echoing with determination and vision.

Dr. Olivia, her gaze alight with possibility, addresses the crowd. "Human-centered financial systems represent a paradigm shift in the way we think about money and finance," she declares. "Instead of prioritizing profits above all else, these systems are designed to serve the needs and aspirations of people, fostering economic inclusion, stability, and well-being for all."

Marcus, his entrepreneurial spirit ignited by the prospect of re-imagining finance, steps forward to share his perspective. "For too long, our financial systems have been driven by greed and speculation, leaving many behind and perpetuating inequality," he proclaims. "But today, we have the opportunity to create a new narrative—to build financial systems that empower individuals, support communities, and promote shared prosperity."

Sofia, her commitment to social justice guiding her words, adds her voice to the conversation. "Human-centered financial systems must prioritize equity and inclusion," she emphasizes. "They should aim to dismantle systemic barriers, expand access to financial services, and ensure that everyone, regardless of background or circumstance, has the opportunity to participate fully in the economy."

As the discussion unfolds, a sense of urgency and possibility fills the room, as participants envision a future where finance serves as a force for good, driving positive social and environmental impact.

In the days and weeks that follow, Dr. Olivia, Marcus, Sofia, and their fellow advocates work tirelessly to advance the principles of human-centered finance in Lusaka. They collaborate with financial institutions to develop products and services that meet the needs of underserved communities, advocate for policies that promote financial inclusion and consumer protection, and raise awareness about the importance of ethical and responsible finance.

Together, they spark a movement for change, inspiring individuals and organizations across the city to embrace a new vision of finance—one that values people over profits, sustainability over short-term gains, and collective well-being over individual wealth.

Their efforts begin to yield results, as financial institutions adopt innovative practices, governments enact progressive policies, and individuals and communities gain greater control over their financial futures. The city begins to transform, becoming a beacon of human-centered finance and a model for others to follow.

And as the impact of human-centered financial systems continues to unfold, a new era of possibility and prosperity dawns in Lusaka—a future where finance serves as a tool for empowerment, a catalyst for social change, and a force for good in the world.

Rethinking Financial Regulation: Putting People First

As the discussion delves deeper into the intricacies of human-centered financial systems, the spotlight shifts to a critical subpoint: rethinking financial regulation—a concept that calls for putting people first in the design and enforcement of financial rules and policies.

Dr. Olivia, Marcus, Sofia, and other advocates stand before the attentive audience, their voices charged with conviction and purpose.

Dr. Olivia, her expertise in economic theory guiding her words, addresses the crowd. "Rethinking financial regulation is essential to creating a financial system that serves the needs of people," she declares. "Instead of focusing solely on stability and profitability, regulations must prioritize consumer protection, equitable access to financial services, and the promotion of sustainable economic growth."

Marcus, his experiences in the business world shaping his perspective, steps forward to share his insights. "For too long, financial regulations have been skewed in favor of powerful institutions, leaving ordinary people vulnerable to exploitation and abuse," he proclaims. "But today, we have the opportunity to change that—to rebalance the scales and ensure that regulations are designed to safeguard the interests of all stakeholders, not just the wealthy few."

Sofia, her advocacy for social justice fueling her passion, adds her voice to the conversation. "Rethinking financial regulation must prioritize equity and inclusion," she emphasizes. "It should aim to address systemic biases and injustices, dismantle barriers to access and opportunity, and hold financial institutions accountable for their actions and impact on society."

As the discussion unfolds, a sense of urgency and determination fills the room, as participants grapple with the complexities of reshaping regulatory frameworks to better serve the needs of people.

In the days and weeks that follow, Dr. Olivia, Marcus, Sofia, and their fellow advocates mobilize to advocate for progressive reforms in financial regulation. They engage with policymakers, regulators, and industry stakeholders to raise awareness about the importance of putting people first in the regulatory process, advocate for policies that promote transparency, fairness, and accountability in financial markets, and push for the adoption of new regulations that prioritize the well-being of consumers and communities.

Together, they form a coalition for change, uniting diverse voices and interests behind a common vision of a financial system that works for everyone.

Their efforts begin to gain traction, as policymakers respond to public pressure and begin to introduce new regulations aimed at curbing predatory practices, promoting responsible lending and investment, and ensuring that financial institutions are held to account for their impact on society.

And as the impact of these reforms begins to be felt, a new era of trust and confidence begins to emerge in the financial system—a system that is no longer seen as a source of instability and inequality, but as a tool for empowerment and progress.

Financial Inclusion: Expanding Access to Financial Services for All

As the discourse delves into the intricacies of human-centered financial systems, the narrative illuminates a crucial subpoint: financial inclusion—an imperative that underscores the need to broaden access to financial services for all members of society.

Dr. Olivia, Marcus, Sofia, and other advocates stand before a diverse assembly, their voices resounding with empathy and resolve.

Dr. Olivia, her expertise in economic theory guiding her assertions, addresses the gathering. "Financial inclusion is not merely an option but a fundamental necessity," she declares. "By extending access to financial services—such as banking, credit, and insurance—we can empower individuals to better manage their finances, invest in their futures, and weather unforeseen challenges."

Marcus, his experiences in entrepreneurship shaping his perspective, steps forward to share his insights. "For too long, financial exclusion has marginalized countless individuals and communities, stifling their potential and perpetuating cycles of poverty," he asserts. "But today, we have the opportunity to change that—to break down barriers and create pathways to economic empowerment for all."

Sofia, her commitment to social justice driving her passion, adds her voice to the conversation. "Financial inclusion must prioritize equity and dignity," she emphasizes. "It should aim to reach marginalized populations, such as women, minorities, and those living in underserved areas, and provide them with the tools and resources they need to participate fully in the economy."

As the dialogue unfolds, a sense of urgency and solidarity permeates the space, as participants grapple with the complexities of expanding financial access to those who have long been overlooked and underserved.

In the ensuing days and weeks, Dr. Olivia, Marcus, Sofia, and their allies mobilize to champion the cause of financial inclusion. They collaborate with financial institutions to develop innovative products and services tailored to the needs of underserved communities, advocate for policies that promote financial literacy and consumer protection, and work to bridge the digital divide by expanding access to digital financial services.

Together, they forge partnerships with grassroots organizations, government agencies, and international stakeholders, uniting their efforts behind a shared vision of a more inclusive and equitable financial system.

Their endeavors begin to yield results, as individuals and families gain access to the financial tools and resources they need to build brighter futures. Bank accounts are opened, loans are secured, and insurance policies are obtained, empowering people to save, invest, and protect themselves against financial shocks.

And as the impact of financial inclusion begins to ripple through society, a new sense of hope and possibility takes hold—a belief that, together, we can create a world where everyone has the opportunity to thrive, regardless of their circumstances.

Consumer Protection in Financial Markets

As the discourse unfolds on the intricacies of human-centered financial systems, the spotlight now shifts to a critical subpoint: consumer protection in financial markets—a pivotal aspect ensuring the safeguarding of individuals against predatory practices and ensuring fair treatment.

Dr. Olivia, Marcus, Sofia, and other advocates stand resolute before the attentive audience, their voices resonating with determination and empathy.

Dr. Olivia, her expertise in economic theory guiding her arguments, steps forward to address the gathering. "Consumer protection is the cornerstone of a just and equitable financial system," she proclaims. "By implementing robust safeguards and regulations, we can ensure that individuals are treated fairly, that their rights are upheld, and that they are shielded from exploitation and abuse."

Marcus, his experiences in entrepreneurship shaping his perspective, echoes her sentiment. "For too long, vulnerable consumers have fallen victim to deceptive practices and predatory lending," he asserts. "But today, we have the opportunity to change that—to enact policies that empower consumers, promote transparency, and hold financial institutions accountable for their actions."

Sofia, her commitment to social justice fueling her passion, adds her voice to the conversation. "Consumer protection must prioritize equity and justice," she emphasizes. "It should aim to address systemic inequalities, protect marginalized communities, and ensure that everyone, regardless of their background or circumstances, can access and use financial services safely and fairly."

As the dialogue intensifies, a sense of urgency and resolve permeates the room, as participants grapple with the complexities of crafting regulations that balance the interests of consumers and financial institutions.

In the ensuing days and weeks, Dr. Olivia, Marcus, Sofia, and their allies mobilize to advocate for stronger consumer protections in financial markets. They engage with policymakers, regulators, and industry stakeholders to raise awareness about the importance of safeguarding consumers' rights, advocate for policies that promote transparency and disclosure, and push for the enforcement of laws that prohibit deceptive practices and abusive behaviors.

Together, they form a coalition for change, united in their commitment to ensuring that consumers are treated fairly and ethically in the financial marketplace.

Their efforts begin to bear fruit, as policymakers respond to public pressure and enact new regulations aimed at protecting consumers from fraud, discrimination, and unfair practices. Financial institutions are held accountable for their actions, and consumers gain greater confidence in the integrity of the financial system.

And as the impact of these reforms begins to be felt, a new era of trust and accountability begins to emerge—a future where consumers can confidently engage with financial markets, secure in the knowledge that their rights and interests are protected.

Sustainable Investing: Aligning Financial Goals with Environmental and Social Objectives

As the discussion on human-centered financial systems unfolds, the focus shifts to a pivotal subpoint: sustainable investing—a concept that underscores the importance of aligning financial goals with environmental and social objectives, ensuring that investments not only generate returns but also contribute to positive impact.

Dr. Olivia, Marcus, Sofia, and other advocates stand before a captivated audience, their voices charged with conviction and purpose.

Dr. Olivia, her expertise in economic theory guiding her words, addresses the gathering. "Sustainable investing represents a paradigm shift in the way we approach finance," she declares. "By integrating environmental, social, and governance (ESG) criteria into investment decisions, we can drive positive change while generating financial returns."

Marcus, his experiences in entrepreneurship shaping his perspective, steps forward to share his insights. "For too long, investors have prioritized short-term gains over long-term sustainability," he asserts. "But today, we have the opportunity to change that—to invest in companies and projects that not only deliver financial value but also create positive social and environmental impact."

Sofia, her commitment to social justice fueling her passion, adds her voice to the conversation. "Sustainable investing must prioritize equity and justice," she emphasizes. "It should aim to address systemic inequalities, support underserved communities, and advance solutions to pressing environmental challenges, such as climate change and resource depletion."

As the dialogue deepens, a sense of urgency and possibility fills the room, as participants grapple with the complexities of reshaping investment practices to better serve people and the planet.

In the ensuing days and weeks, Dr. Olivia, Marcus, Sofia, and their allies mobilize to promote sustainable investing in Lusaka. They engage with investors, asset managers, and financial advisors to raise awareness about the benefits of incorporating ESG factors into investment decisions, advocate for policies that incentivize sustainable finance, and work to build a robust ecosystem of sustainable investment opportunities.

Together, they form a coalition for change, united in their commitment to harnessing the power of finance for good.

Their efforts begin to gain traction, as investors increasingly recognize the value of sustainable investing and incorporate ESG considerations into their portfolios. Companies are held accountable for their environmental and social impact, and sustainable projects receive the funding they need to thrive.

And as the impact of sustainable investing begins to ripple through society, a new era of possibility and prosperity takes hold—a future where finance is a force for positive change, where investments generate returns while also creating lasting value for people and the planet.

Fintech and Innovation in Financial Services

As the discourse on human-centered financial systems continues, the conversation pivots to a critical subpoint: fintech and innovation in financial services—a realm where technological advancements intersect with finance to revolutionize the way

CHAPTER TEN: HUMAN-CENTERED FINANCIAL SYSTEMS

people access and manage their money.

Dr. Olivia, Marcus, Sofia, and other advocates stand poised before an eager audience, their voices resonating with anticipation and possibility.

Dr. Olivia, her expertise in economic theory guiding her arguments, steps forward to address the crowd. "Fintech represents a transformative opportunity to democratize finance," she declares. "By leveraging technology, we can expand access to financial services, lower costs, and empower individuals to take control of their financial futures."

Marcus, his entrepreneurial spirit ignited by the prospect of innovation, adds his perspective. "For too long, traditional financial services have been inaccessible and outdated," he asserts. "But today, we have the opportunity to change that—to harness the power of fintech to create more inclusive, efficient, and responsive financial systems."

Sofia, her commitment to social justice driving her passion, emphasizes the importance of ensuring that fintech innovations prioritize equity and inclusion. "Fintech must not only benefit the few but uplift the many," she proclaims. "It should aim to reach underserved communities, bridge the digital divide, and address the unique needs and challenges faced by marginalized populations."

As the dialogue unfolds, a sense of excitement and possibility fills the room, as participants envision the transformative potential of fintech to reshape the financial landscape.

In the ensuing days and weeks, Dr. Olivia, Marcus, Sofia, and their allies mobilize to promote fintech innovation in Lusaka. They collaborate with tech startups, financial institutions, and regulatory bodies to foster an ecosystem that supports fintech development, advocate for policies that promote innovation and consumer protection, and work to ensure that fintech solutions are accessible and inclusive for all members of society.

Together, they form a coalition for change, united in their belief that technology can be a force for good in the world of finance.

Their efforts begin to yield results, as fintech solutions proliferate, offering new ways for individuals to manage their finances, access credit, and invest in their futures. Digital banking platforms emerge, offering affordable and convenient services to previously underserved communities. And innovative financial products, such as microloans and peer-to-peer lending, empower entrepreneurs and small businesses to thrive.

And as the impact of fintech innovation begins to be felt, a new era of possibility and progress takes hold—a future where finance is more accessible, inclusive, and responsive to the needs of people.

Building Resilient Financial Systems: Lessons from Crisis Management

Amidst the discourse on human-centered financial systems, the narrative now shifts to a crucial subpoint: building resilient financial systems—a theme underscored by the imperative of drawing lessons from crisis management to fortify the stability and sustainability of financial markets.

Dr. Olivia, Marcus, Sofia, and other advocates stand poised before an engaged audience, their voices echoing with determination and foresight.

Dr. Olivia, her mastery of economic theory guiding her

insights, steps forward to address the gathering. "Building resilient financial systems is essential to safeguarding against future crises," she asserts. "By analyzing past failures and implementing robust risk management measures, we can better protect individuals and communities from the devastating impacts of financial instability."

Marcus, his entrepreneurial acumen honed by adversity, adds his perspective. "For too long, financial systems have been plagued by cycles of boom and bust," he declares. "But today, we have the opportunity to break that cycle—to strengthen our defenses and build systems that are capable of withstanding shocks and disruptions."

Sofia, her dedication to social justice fueling her resolve, emphasizes the importance of ensuring that resilient financial systems prioritize equity and inclusion. "Resilience must not come at the expense of vulnerable communities," she asserts. "It should aim to build systems that are not only robust but also fair and just, ensuring that everyone has access to the support and resources they need to weather financial storms."

As the dialogue unfolds, a sense of urgency and solidarity permeates the room, as participants grapple with the complexities of fortifying financial systems against future crises.

In the ensuing days and weeks, Dr. Olivia, Marcus, Sofia, and their allies mobilize to advocate for resilience in Lusaka's financial systems. They collaborate with policymakers, regulators, and industry stakeholders to identify weaknesses and vulnerabilities, advocate for reforms that strengthen oversight and accountability, and work to build a culture of risk awareness and preparedness.

Together, they form a coalition for change, united in their commitment to building financial systems that are not only resilient but also equitable and just.

Their efforts begin to bear fruit, as policymakers and regulators take action to implement reforms that strengthen the stability and sustainability of financial markets. Risk management practices are improved, regulatory frameworks are updated, and financial institutions are held to higher standards of accountability.

And as the impact of these efforts begins to be felt, a new era of confidence and stability begins to emerge—a future where financial systems are no longer a source of fear and uncertainty, but a source of strength and resilience.

11

Chapter eleven: Psychology of Economic Policy

In the heart of Lusaka, where the pulse of economic policy beats relentlessly, a gathering of policymakers, economists, and advocates convenes to explore the intricate interplay between human psychology and economic decision-making.

Dr. Olivia, Marcus, Sofia, and other luminaries stand at the forefront of the discourse, their voices poised to illuminate the complexities of shaping policy in a world driven by human behavior.

Dr. Olivia, her scholarly insights guiding her discourse, addresses the assembly with gravitas. "The psychology of economic policy is a nuanced dance between rationality and emotion," she begins. "Understanding how individuals perceive and respond to policy interventions is essential to crafting effective strategies that promote economic stability and prosperity."

Marcus, his entrepreneurial spirit infusing his perspective, steps forward to share his experiences. "For too long, economic policies have been designed without fully accounting for the psychological factors that influence behavior," he contends. "But today, we have the opportunity to change that—to leverage insights from psychology to design policies that resonate with people's values, beliefs, and aspirations."

Sofia, her advocacy for social justice fueling her passion, adds her voice to the conversation. "The psychology of economic policy must prioritize empathy and compassion," she emphasizes. "It should aim to understand the lived experiences of individuals and communities affected by policy decisions, and strive to create policies that promote fairness, equity, and social cohesion."

As the dialogue unfolds, a tapestry of perspectives and insights emerges, weaving together the intricate threads of human psychology and economic policy.

In the days and weeks that follow, Dr. Olivia, Marcus, Sofia, and their allies mobilize to advocate for a more psychologically informed approach to economic policy in Lusaka. They engage with policymakers, researchers, and community leaders to raise awareness about the importance of considering psychological factors in policy design, advocate for policies that promote well-being and resilience, and work to build a culture of evidence-based policy making that values the voices and experiences of all citizens.

Together, they form a coalition for change, united in their commitment to shaping economic policies that not only drive growth and prosperity but also nurture the human spirit and enhance the quality of life for all.

Their efforts begin to yield results, as policymakers embrace a more holistic approach to economic policy that incorporates insights from psychology into decision-making processes.

Policies are redesigned to better align with people's values and motivations, and initiatives are launched to promote financial literacy, mental health, and social cohesion.

And as the impact of these efforts begins to be felt, a new era of possibility and progress dawns—a future where economic policies are not just numbers on a spreadsheet, but instruments of positive change that uplift and empower individuals and communities.

The Behavioral Economics of Policy Design

As the discussion delves deeper into the psychology of economic policy, the spotlight now shines on a pivotal subpoint: the behavioral economics of policy design—a realm where insights from psychology intersect with economic theory to inform the crafting of more effective and impactful policies.

Dr. Olivia, Marcus, Sofia, and other thought leaders stand before an attentive audience, their voices resonating with determination and innovation.

Dr. Olivia, her expertise in economic theory guiding her discourse, steps forward to address the gathering. "The behavioral economics of policy design offers a fresh perspective on how individuals make decisions," she begins. "By recognizing and accounting for cognitive biases and heuristics, policymakers can design interventions that nudge people towards better outcomes and enhance the effectiveness of policy initiatives."

Marcus, his entrepreneurial mindset sparking his insights, adds his perspective to the conversation. "For too long, policymakers have relied on outdated models of human behavior," he asserts. "But today, we have the opportunity to embrace the principles of behavioral economics—to design policies that acknowledge the limitations of human rationality and leverage behavioral insights to drive positive change."

Sofia, her commitment to social justice driving her passion, emphasizes the importance of ensuring that policies designed with behavioral insights prioritize equity and inclusion. "Behavioral economics must not perpetuate inequalities," she insists. "It should aim to understand the unique challenges faced by different groups within society and design interventions that promote fairness, justice, and empowerment for all."

As the dialogue unfolds, a sense of excitement and possibility fills the room, as participants grapple with the implications of applying behavioral insights to policy design.

In the ensuing days and weeks, Dr. Olivia, Marcus, Sofia, and their allies mobilize to advocate for the integration of behavioral economics into policy-making processes in Lusaka. They collaborate with policymakers, researchers, and community stakeholders to raise awareness about the potential of behavioral insights to inform policy design, advocate for the adoption of evidence-based approaches to decision-making, and work to build capacity for behavioral analysis within government institutions.

Together, they form a coalition for change, united in their commitment to shaping policies that not only reflect the realities of human behavior but also harness the power of behavioral insights to improve outcomes for individuals and society as a whole.

Their efforts begin to yield results, as policymakers embrace behavioral economics as a valuable tool for designing more effective and equitable policies. Nudge interventions are implemented to encourage healthier behaviors, simplify decision-making processes, and promote financial well-being. And initiatives are launched to address behavioral barriers to participation in social programs, such as access to education and healthcare.

And as the impact of these efforts begins to be felt, a new era of possibility and progress takes hold—a future where policies are designed with a deep understanding of human behavior, where interventions are tailored to the needs and preferences of individuals, and where government works in partnership with citizens to create a more just, equitable, and compassionate society.

Public Opinion and Policy Making: Understanding Citizen Preferences

In the symphony of economic policy, a new movement emerges, focused on the intersection of public opinion and policy-making—a theme that emphasizes the importance of understanding citizen preferences to inform more responsive and democratic governance.

Dr. Olivia, Marcus, Sofia, and other influential voices gather once more, their faces alight with anticipation as they prepare to delve into the complexities of this critical subpoint.

Dr. Olivia, her scholarly acumen guiding her discourse, steps forward to address the assembly. "Public opinion plays a pivotal role in shaping economic policy," she begins. "By listening to the voices of citizens and understanding their preferences, policymakers can ensure that policies are not only effective but also reflect the values and aspirations of the people they serve."

Marcus, his experiences in entrepreneurship lending depth

to his perspective, adds his voice to the conversation. "For too long, policy-making has been disconnected from the realities of everyday life," he asserts. "But today, we have the opportunity to bridge that gap—to engage with citizens, solicit their feedback, and involve them in the decision-making process to create policies that truly resonate with their needs and desires."

Sofia, her dedication to social justice infusing her passion, emphasizes the importance of ensuring that public opinion and policy-making prioritize equity and inclusion. "Public opinion must not be a privilege reserved for the few," she declares. "It should aim to amplify the voices of marginalized communities, empower citizens to shape their own destinies, and hold policymakers accountable for their actions."

As the dialogue unfolds, a sense of urgency and possibility fills the room, as participants grapple with the complexities of translating public sentiment into meaningful policy action.

In the ensuing days and weeks, Dr. Olivia, Marcus, Sofia, and their allies mobilize to advocate for greater transparency, participation, and accountability in policy-making processes in Lusaka. They engage with citizens, community organizations, and advocacy groups to gather input on policy priorities, facilitate dialogue between stakeholders, and advocate for reforms that strengthen democratic governance and civic engagement.

Together, they form a coalition for change, united in their commitment to shaping policies that not only reflect the will of the people but also empower citizens to participate in the decisions that affect their lives.

Their efforts begin to yield results, as policymakers embrace a more inclusive and participatory approach to policy-making.

Town hall meetings are held to solicit input on key policy issues, online platforms are launched to facilitate public engagement, and citizens are invited to serve on advisory committees and task forces to provide input on policy development and implementation.

And as the impact of these efforts begins to be felt, a new era of civic empowerment and democratic renewal takes hold—a future where citizens are not just passive recipients of policy decisions, but active participants in shaping the future of their communities and their country.

Political Economy; Analyzing the Interplay Between Economics and Politics

As the discussion on human-centered financial systems unfolds, the spotlight now turns to a crucial subpoint: political economy—an exploration of the intricate interplay between economics and politics, where decisions are shaped not just by economic theory, but by the dynamics of power, ideology, and governance.

Dr. Olivia, Marcus, Sofia, and other influential figures gather once more, their faces etched with determination as they prepare to unravel the complexities of this pivotal subtopic.

Dr. Olivia, her scholarly expertise guiding her discourse, steps forward to address the assembly. "Political economy is the nexus where economic theory meets the realities of power and governance," she begins. "Understanding this interplay is essential for crafting policies that are not only economically sound but also politically viable."

Marcus, his experiences in navigating the intersection of

business and politics lending depth to his perspective, adds his voice to the conversation. "For too long, economic policies have been shaped by political expediency rather than economic rationale," he asserts. "But today, we have the opportunity to challenge that paradigm—to advocate for policies that prioritize the common good over partisan interests and ideological divides."

Sofia, her dedication to social justice infusing her passion, emphasizes the importance of ensuring that political economy analysis prioritizes equity and inclusion. "Political economy must not perpetuate inequalities or serve the interests of the few," she declares. "It should aim to understand the power dynamics that shape economic policies and work to ensure that decision-making processes are transparent, accountable, and inclusive of all voices."

As the dialogue unfolds, a sense of urgency and possibility fills the room, as participants grapple with the complexities of navigating the intersection of economics and politics in the pursuit of a more just and equitable society.

In the ensuing days and weeks, Dr. Olivia, Marcus, Sofia, and their allies mobilize to advocate for a more transparent, accountable, and inclusive approach to political economy analysis in Lusaka. They engage with policymakers, civil society organizations, and grassroots movements to raise awareness about the importance of considering power dynamics in economic decision-making, advocate for reforms that promote transparency and accountability in governance, and work to build coalitions that bridge ideological divides and promote the common good.

Together, they form a coalition for change, united in their commitment to shaping political and economic systems that serve the interests of all members of society, not just the privileged few.

Their efforts begin to yield results, as policymakers embrace a more inclusive and participatory approach to political economy analysis. Decision-making processes become more transparent, special interests are held to account, and policies are crafted with greater consideration for their impact on marginalized communities.

And as the impact of these efforts begins to be felt, a new era of possibility and progress takes hold—a future where political and economic systems are not just instruments of power and privilege, but tools for promoting justice, equality, and human dignity.

Behavioral Public Administration: Improving Government Effectiveness Through Psychological Insights

As the discourse on human-centered financial systems unfolds, attention turns to a critical subpoint: behavioral public administration—a domain where insights from psychology are leveraged to enhance government effectiveness and improve public services.

In the heart of Lusaka's administrative hub, Dr. Olivia, Marcus, Sofia, and other luminaries gather once more, their minds ablaze with the possibilities of applying psychological insights to governance.

Dr. Olivia, her scholarly rigor guiding her discourse, steps forward to address the assembly. "Behavioral public administration offers a paradigm shift in how we approach governance," she begins. "By understanding the cognitive biases and decision-making heuristics that influence both policymakers and citizens, we can design more effective public policies and deliver better outcomes for all."

Marcus, his experiences in navigating the intersection of business and government lending depth to his perspective, adds his voice to the conversation. "For too long, government agencies have operated under the assumption of rational decision-making," he asserts. "But today, we have the opportunity to embrace a more nuanced understanding of human behavior—to design interventions that nudge policymakers and citizens towards better decisions and more effective outcomes."

Sofia, her dedication to social justice fueling her passion, emphasizes the importance of ensuring that behavioral public administration prioritizes equity and inclusion. "Behavioral insights must not be used to manipulate or coerce," she declares. "They should aim to empower citizens, enhance transparency and accountability, and promote the well-being of all members of society."

As the dialogue unfolds, a sense of optimism and possibility fills the room, as participants grapple with the potential of applying psychological insights to transform governance and public administration.

In the days and weeks that follow, Dr. Olivia, Marcus, Sofia, and their allies mobilize to advocate for the integration of behavioral insights into government decision-making processes. They engage with public officials, civil servants, and community leaders to raise awareness about the value of behavioral public administration, advocate for the adoption of evidence-based approaches to policy design and implementation, and work to build capacity for behavioral analysis within government agencies.

Together, they form a coalition for change, united in their commitment to shaping governance systems that are more responsive, inclusive, and effective.

Their efforts begin to yield results, as government agencies embrace behavioral insights as a valuable tool for improving service delivery and enhancing public trust. Nudge interventions are implemented to encourage compliance with regulations, simplify bureaucratic processes, and promote citizen engagement. And initiatives are launched to address behavioral barriers to participation in public programs, such as access to education, healthcare, and social services.

And as the impact of these efforts begins to be felt, a new era of possibility and progress takes hold—a future where governance is not just about rules and regulations, but about understanding and responding to the needs and aspirations of the people.

Policy Evaluation: Incorporating Behavioral Metrics into Assessment Frameworks

In the bustling halls of policy institutions, a new wave of thought emerges, focusing on the critical subpoint of policy evaluation—a realm where behavioral metrics are integrated into assessment frameworks to provide a more nuanced understanding of policy effectiveness.

Dr. Olivia, Marcus, Sofia, and other influential figures convene once more, their minds ablaze with the potential of incorporating behavioral insights into policy evaluation.

Dr. Olivia, her scholarly rigor guiding her discourse, steps forward to address the assembly. "Policy evaluation is the cornerstone of effective governance," she begins. "By incorporating behavioral metrics into assessment frameworks, we can gain deeper insights into how policies impact the behavior and well-being of individuals and communities."

Marcus, his experiences in navigating the complexities of business strategy lending depth to his perspective, adds his voice to the conversation. "For too long, policy evaluation has relied solely on traditional metrics of success," he asserts. "But today, we have the opportunity to embrace a more holistic approach—to assess policies not just by their economic impact, but by their ability to address the diverse needs and preferences of the people they serve."

Sofia, her dedication to social justice fueling her passion, emphasizes the importance of ensuring that policy evaluation prioritizes equity and inclusion. "Policy evaluation must not perpetuate inequalities or marginalize vulnerable communities," she declares. "It should aim to understand the social and cultural context in which policies operate, and to assess their impact on different groups within society."

As the dialogue unfolds, a sense of urgency and possibility fills the room, as participants grapple with the complexities of integrating behavioral metrics into policy evaluation frameworks.

In the ensuing days and weeks, Dr. Olivia, Marcus, Sofia, and their allies mobilize to advocate for the adoption of more inclusive and comprehensive approaches to policy evaluation. They engage with policymakers, researchers, and civil society organizations to raise awareness about the value of incorporating behavioral insights into assessment frameworks, advocate for the development of new methodologies and tools for measuring policy impact, and work to build capacity for behavioral analysis within evaluation processes.

Together, they form a coalition for change, united in their commitment to shaping policy evaluation systems that are more responsive, transparent, and equitable.

Their efforts begin to yield results, as policymakers embrace a more holistic approach to assessing policy effectiveness. Evaluation frameworks are updated to include a broader range of indicators, including measures of well-being, social cohesion, and equity. And initiatives are launched to involve stakeholders in the evaluation process, ensuring that the voices and experiences of all members of society are heard and valued.

And as the impact of these efforts begins to be felt, a new era of possibility and progress takes hold—a future where policy evaluation is not just a technical exercise, but a transformative tool for building a more just, equitable, and inclusive society.

Ethical Considerations in Policy Implementation: Balancing Efficiency with Equity

In the corridors of power, a critical subpoint emerges amidst the discussions on human-centered financial systems: ethical considerations in policy implementation—a domain where the delicate balance between efficiency and equity takes center stage.

Dr. Olivia, Marcus, Sofia, and other influential figures gather once more, their faces etched with resolve as they grapple with the complexities of ethical decision-making in governance.

Dr. Olivia, her scholarly acumen guiding her discourse, steps forward to address the assembly. "Ethical considerations lie at the heart of effective policy implementation," she begins.

"As stewards of public trust, policymakers must navigate the tension between efficiency and equity, ensuring that policies not only achieve their intended outcomes but also uphold principles of fairness, justice, and human dignity."

Marcus, drawing from his experiences in the business world, adds his perspective to the conversation. "For too long, policymakers have prioritized short-term gains over long-term sustainability," he asserts. "But today, we have the opportunity to embrace a more ethical approach—to design and implement policies that not only drive economic growth but also promote social cohesion and environmental stewardship."

Sofia, her dedication to social justice infusing her passion, emphasizes the importance of ensuring that policy implementation prioritizes equity and inclusion. "Policy implementation must not exacerbate existing inequalities or perpetuate systemic injustices," she declares. "It should aim to address the needs and aspirations of all members of society, particularly those who have been historically marginalized or excluded."

As the dialogue unfolds, a sense of urgency and conviction fills the room, as participants grapple with the ethical dilemmas inherent in policy implementation.

In the ensuing days and weeks, Dr. Olivia, Marcus, Sofia, and their allies mobilize to advocate for a more ethical approach to policy implementation. They engage with policymakers, civil society organizations, and grassroots movements to raise awareness about the importance of ethical decision-making in governance, advocate for reforms that prioritize equity and justice, and work to build coalitions that bridge ideological divides and promote the common good.

Together, they form a coalition for change, united in their commitment to shaping policies that are not only effective but also ethical.

Their efforts begin to yield results, as policymakers embrace a more principled approach to policy implementation. Decision-making processes become more transparent, accountability mechanisms are strengthened, and policies are crafted with greater consideration for their impact on vulnerable communities.

And as the impact of these efforts begins to be felt, a new era of possibility and progress takes hold—a future where policy implementation is not just about achieving objectives, but about upholding values and principles that reflect the best aspirations of humanity.

12

Chapter Twelve: Cultural Economics and Creative Industries

In the vibrant heart of Lusaka, where the pulse of creativity beats in rhythm with the city's diverse culture, a new chapter unfolds—a journey into the realm of cultural economics and the creative industries.

Dr. Olivia, Marcus, Sofia, and other luminaries gather once more, their spirits lifted by the promise of exploring the intersection of economics and culture.

Dr. Olivia, her scholarly curiosity guiding her discourse, steps forward to address the assembly. "Cultural economics offers a unique lens through which to understand the value of artistic expression and cultural heritage," she begins. "By examining the economic dimensions of cultural production and consumption, we can unlock new opportunities for creativity, innovation, and economic growth."

Marcus, his passion for entrepreneurship ignited by the city's dynamic arts scene, adds his perspective to the conversation. "For too long, the creative industries have been undervalued and underappreciated," he asserts. "But today, we have the opportunity to celebrate the economic and social contributions of artists, musicians, writers, and cultural entrepreneurs—to recognize that creativity is not just a luxury, but a fundamental driver of human progress and prosperity."

Sofia, her commitment to social justice intertwined with her love for the arts, emphasizes the importance of ensuring that cultural economics prioritizes equity and inclusion. "The arts have the power to unite us across divides of race, class, and nationality," she declares. "But we must also recognize that not all voices have been heard or valued equally in the cultural marketplace. It is our responsibility to promote diversity, equity, and representation in the creative industries, ensuring that everyone has the opportunity to participate in and benefit from cultural expression."

As the dialogue unfolds, a sense of wonder and possibility fills the room, as participants grapple with the complexities of valuing and supporting the arts in a rapidly changing world.

In the days and weeks that follow, Dr. Olivia, Marcus, Sofia, and their allies mobilize to advocate for the recognition and support of the creative industries in Lusaka. They engage with policymakers, cultural organizations, and community groups to raise awareness about the economic and social value of the arts, advocate for policies and investments that promote creativity and cultural expression, and work to build bridges between artists, entrepreneurs, and audiences.

Together, they form a coalition for change, united in their commitment to fostering a vibrant and inclusive cultural ecosystem that celebrates the diversity and richness of human expression.

Their efforts begin to yield results, as policymakers embrace the economic potential of the creative industries and invest in initiatives that support artistic innovation, cultural preservation, and community engagement. New partnerships are forged between artists and businesses, cultural institutions and educational organizations, and government agencies and grassroots initiatives, creating a thriving ecosystem where creativity can flourish and thrive.

And as the impact of these efforts begins to be felt, a new era of possibility and progress takes hold—a future where the arts are not just a reflection of our humanity, but a catalyst for economic growth, social cohesion, and cultural renewal.

Cultural Capital: The Role of Arts and Culture in Economic Development

As the discussion on cultural economics and the creative industries unfolds, attention turns to a critical subpoint: cultural capital—the role of arts and culture in economic development, where the richness of Lusaka's cultural tapestry emerges as a driving force for prosperity and growth.

Dr. Olivia, Marcus, Sofia, and other influential figures reconvene, their minds ablaze with the possibilities of harnessing the city's cultural wealth for economic advancement.

Dr. Olivia, her scholarly insights illuminating her discourse, steps forward to address the assembly. "Cultural capital encompasses the tangible and intangible assets that contribute to the vibrancy and vitality of a community," she begins. "From museums and theaters to festivals and street art, the arts and culture sector not only enriches our lives but also drives economic activity, tourism, and innovation."

Marcus, his entrepreneurial spirit ignited by the city's diverse cultural offerings, adds his perspective to the conversation. "For too long, the economic potential of the arts has been underestimated," he asserts. "But today, we have the opportunity to leverage our cultural capital as a strategic asset—to attract investment, talent, and visitors, and to position Lusaka as a global hub for creativity and innovation."

Sofia, her passion for social justice intertwined with her love for the arts, emphasizes the importance of ensuring that cultural capital benefits all members of society. "The arts have the power to bring people together, to foster understanding and empathy, and to bridge divides," she declares. "But we must also ensure that the benefits of cultural development are shared equitably, particularly in underserved and marginalized communities."

As the dialogue unfolds, a sense of excitement and possibility fills the room, as participants grapple with the transformative potential of cultural capital in driving economic development and social progress.

In the days and weeks that follow, Dr. Olivia, Marcus, Sofia, and their allies mobilize to advocate for the recognition and investment in Lusaka's cultural capital. They engage with policymakers, urban planners, business leaders, and community activists to develop strategies for leveraging the city's cultural assets, advocate for policies and investments that support arts education, cultural infrastructure, and creative entrepreneurship, and work to ensure that cultural development benefits all residents, regardless of background or socioeconomic status.

Together, they form a coalition for change, united in their commitment to harnessing the power of arts and culture to build a more vibrant, inclusive, and prosperous Lusaka.

Their efforts begin to yield results, as policymakers embrace the economic and social value of cultural capital and invest in initiatives that support artistic expression, cultural preservation, and community engagement. Cultural districts emerge as hubs of creativity and innovation, attracting artists, entrepreneurs, and visitors from around the world. And partnerships are forged between the public and private sectors, cultural institutions, and community organizations, creating a collaborative ecosystem where creativity can thrive and flourish.

And as the impact of these efforts begins to be felt, a new era of possibility and progress takes hold—a future where Lusaka's cultural capital is not just a source of pride and inspiration, but a catalyst for economic growth, social cohesion, and human flourishing.

Economics of Creativity: Understanding the Value of Intellectual Property

In the corridors of creativity and innovation, a critical subpoint emerges amidst the discussions on cultural economics and the creative industries: the economics of creativity—the intricate dance between artistry and commerce, where the value of intellectual property takes center stage.

Dr. Olivia, Marcus, Sofia, and other influential figures reconvene, their minds buzzing with the complexities of valuing and protecting creative works in a rapidly evolving digital landscape.

Dr. Olivia, her scholarly expertise guiding her discourse, steps forward to address the assembly. "The economics of creativity delves into the intricacies of intellectual property rights—the legal and economic frameworks that govern the ownership and exploitation of artistic and cultural works," she begins. "From music and film to literature and design, intellectual property plays a central role in incentivizing creativity, rewarding innovation, and fostering economic growth."

Marcus, his experiences in the world of entrepreneurship lending depth to his perspective, adds his voice to the conversation. "For too long, creators have struggled to secure fair compensation for their work in the digital age," he asserts. "But today, we have the opportunity to re-imagine the economics of creativity—to develop new models and technologies that protect and empower artists, while also ensuring that consumers have access to a diverse range of cultural expressions."

Sofia, her passion for social justice infusing her advocacy, emphasizes the importance of ensuring that the economics of creativity prioritizes equity and inclusion. "The digital revolution has transformed the way we create, distribute, and consume cultural content," she declares. "But we must also ensure that these changes benefit all members of society, particularly marginalized and underrepresented communities, who have historically been excluded from traditional creative industries."

As the dialogue unfolds, a sense of urgency and possibility fills the room, as participants grapple with the challenges and opportunities presented by the economics of creativity.

In the ensuing days and weeks, Dr. Olivia, Marcus, Sofia, and their allies mobilize to advocate for a more equitable and sustainable approach to intellectual property rights. They engage with policymakers, legal experts, technology innovators, and cultural practitioners to develop strategies for protecting and promoting creativity in the digital age, advocate for reforms that balance the interests of creators, consumers, and society at large, and work to build coalitions that bridge the divide between traditional and emerging creative industries.

Together, they form a coalition for change, united in their commitment to shaping an economy of creativity that is fair, inclusive, and conducive to artistic innovation and cultural diversity.

Their efforts begin to yield results, as policymakers embrace new approaches to intellectual property rights that prioritize the rights of creators while also promoting access to cultural content. Copyright laws are updated to reflect the realities of the digital age, ensuring that artists are fairly compensated for their work and that cultural heritage is preserved and protected for future generations. And initiatives are launched to promote digital literacy and creative entrepreneurship, empowering individuals from all backgrounds to participate in and benefit from the creative economy.

And as the impact of these efforts begins to be felt, a new era of possibility and progress takes hold—a future where the economics of creativity is not just about profit and protection, but about fostering a culture of innovation, expression, and belonging.

Cultural Policy: Supporting Arts and Heritage Preservation

As the discussion on human-centered financial systems continues, attention shifts to a crucial subpoint: cultural policy—the strategic framework for supporting arts and heritage preservation, where the preservation of cultural identity intersects with economic sustainability.

Dr. Olivia, Marcus, Sofia, and other influential figures reconvene, their minds focused on the intricate balance between cultural preservation and economic development.

Dr. Olivia, her scholarly expertise guiding her discourse, steps forward to address the assembly. "Cultural policy plays a vital role in shaping the cultural landscape of our city," she begins. "It encompasses a range of measures aimed at promoting artistic expression, preserving cultural heritage, and fostering creative industries—all while ensuring the long-term sustainability of our cultural ecosystem."

Marcus, drawing from his experiences in entrepreneurship and the arts, adds his perspective to the conversation. "For too long, cultural policy has been seen as separate from economic policy," he asserts. "But today, we have the opportunity to integrate cultural considerations into our financial systems—to recognize the intrinsic value of arts and heritage preservation, not just as expressions of our identity, but as drivers of economic growth and community well-being."

Sofia, her passion for social justice intertwined with her advocacy for the arts, emphasizes the importance of ensuring that cultural policy benefits all members of society. "The arts have the power to uplift and empower communities," she declares. "But we must also ensure that cultural policies are inclusive and accessible, particularly for marginalized and underrepresented groups, who have historically been excluded from cultural institutions and opportunities."

As the dialogue unfolds, a sense of urgency and possibility fills the room, as participants grapple with the complexities of crafting cultural policy that balances economic imperatives with cultural preservation.

In the days and weeks that follow, Dr. Olivia, Marcus, Sofia, and their allies mobilize to advocate for a more holistic approach to cultural policy. They engage with policymakers, cultural organizations, community groups, and indigenous communities to develop strategies for promoting cultural diversity, supporting artistic innovation, and preserving heritage sites and traditions. They advocate for increased funding for arts education, cultural infrastructure, and creative entrepreneurship, and work to ensure that cultural policy reflects the needs and aspirations of all residents, regardless of background or socioeconomic status.

Together, they form a coalition for change, united in their commitment to harnessing the power of cultural policy to build a more vibrant, inclusive, and culturally rich city.

Their efforts begin to yield results, as policymakers embrace a more integrated approach to cultural policy that recognizes the economic, social, and cultural value of the arts and heritage preservation. New partnerships are forged between government agencies, cultural institutions, and community organizations, creating a collaborative ecosystem where creativity can thrive and flourish. And initiatives are launched to promote cultural tourism, creative placemaking, and cultural exchange, fostering connections and understanding between diverse communities and cultures.

And as the impact of these efforts begins to be felt, a new era of possibility and progress takes hold—a future where cultural policy is not just about preserving the past, but about shaping the future—a future where arts and heritage preservation are celebrated as essential elements of our city's identity, economy, and social fabric.

Tourism Economics: Harnessing Cultural Resources for Economic Growth

Amidst the exploration of cultural economics and the creative industries, a pivotal subpoint emerges: tourism economics—the strategic utilization of cultural resources for economic growth, where the allure of heritage intersects with the promise of prosperity.

Dr. Olivia, Marcus, Sofia, and other influential figures reconvene, their minds abuzz with the potential of leveraging cultural assets to drive tourism and economic development.

Dr. Olivia, her scholarly acumen guiding her discourse, steps forward to address the assembly. "Tourism economics represents a unique opportunity to showcase our city's rich cultural heritage to the world," she begins. "By capitalizing on our unique attractions, from historic landmarks to cultural festivals, we can attract visitors, stimulate economic activity, and enhance the overall quality of life for residents."

Marcus, drawing from his experiences in entrepreneurship and tourism, adds his perspective to the conversation. "For too long, we've underestimated the economic potential of cultural tourism," he asserts. "But today, we have the opportunity to position our city as a premier destination for cultural travelers—to offer authentic experiences that celebrate our heritage, support local businesses, and create jobs."

Sofia, her passion for social justice intertwined with her advocacy for the arts, emphasizes the importance of ensuring that tourism benefits all members of society. "Tourism has the power to uplift and empower communities," she declares. "But we must also ensure that it is sustainable and equitable, that it respects local cultures and traditions, and that it benefits residents as much as it does visitors."

As the dialogue unfolds, a sense of excitement and possibility fills the room, as participants grapple with the complexities of harnessing cultural resources for tourism while preserving their authenticity and integrity.

In the days and weeks that follow, Dr. Olivia, Marcus, Sofia, and their allies mobilize to advocate for a more responsible and inclusive approach to cultural tourism. They engage with policymakers, tourism operators, cultural institutions, and community groups to develop strategies for promoting sustainable tourism practices, supporting local artisans and entrepreneurs, and preserving cultural heritage sites and traditions. They advocate for investments in tourism infrastructure, marketing campaigns that highlight the city's unique cultural offerings, and initiatives that foster cultural exchange and understanding between visitors and residents.

Together, they form a coalition for change, united in their commitment to harnessing the power of cultural tourism to build a more vibrant, inclusive, and economically prosperous city.

Their efforts begin to yield results, as policymakers embrace a more sustainable and inclusive approach to tourism development. New partnerships are forged between the public and private sectors, cultural organizations, and community groups, creating a collaborative ecosystem where tourism can be a force for positive change. And initiatives are launched to promote community-based tourism, support cultural festivals and events, and preserve heritage sites and traditions for future generations.

And as the impact of these efforts begins to be felt, a new era of possibility and progress takes hold—a future where cultural tourism is not just about attracting visitors, but about celebrating our shared humanity, preserving our cultural heritage, and building bridges of understanding and appreciation between diverse communities and cultures.

Digital Culture and the Creative Economy

Within the realm of cultural economics and creative industries, a new subpoint emerges: digital culture and the creative economy—the convergence of technology and creativity, where digital innovation opens doors to unprecedented opportunities for artistic expression and economic growth.

Dr. Olivia, Marcus, Sofia, and other influential figures reconvene, their minds ignited by the possibilities of the digital age and its impact on cultural production and consumption.

Dr. Olivia, her scholarly insights guiding her discourse, steps forward to address the assembly. "Digital culture represents a paradigm shift in the way we create, distribute, and consume cultural content," she begins. "From online platforms to virtual reality experiences, digital technology has revolutionized the creative economy, offering new avenues for artists and entrepreneurs to reach global audiences and monetize their work."

Marcus, drawing from his experiences as both an

entrepreneur and a consumer of digital content, adds his perspective to the conversation. "For too long, the digital realm has been seen as a threat to traditional cultural industries," he asserts. "But today, we have the opportunity to embrace digital culture as a catalyst for innovation and growth—to harness the power of technology to democratize access to culture, empower creators, and build sustainable business models for the creative economy."

Sofia, her passion for social justice intertwined with her advocacy for the arts, emphasizes the importance of ensuring that digital culture benefits all members of society. "The digital divide is real," she declares. "But we must also ensure that digital culture is accessible and inclusive, that it reflects the diversity of human experience, and that it empowers communities to tell their own stories and shape their own narratives."

As the dialogue unfolds, a sense of excitement and apprehension fills the room, as participants grapple with the opportunities and challenges presented by the digital revolution.

In the days and weeks that follow, Dr. Olivia, Marcus, Sofia, and their allies mobilize to advocate for a more equitable and sustainable approach to digital culture. They engage with policymakers, technology companies, cultural institutions, and community organizations to develop strategies for promoting digital literacy, supporting digital creators and entrepreneurs, and ensuring that digital platforms and content reflect the interests and values of diverse communities.

Together, they form a coalition for change, united in their commitment to harnessing the power of digital culture to build a more vibrant, inclusive, and economically prosperous society.

Their efforts begin to yield results, as policymakers embrace policies and initiatives that promote digital inclusion, support digital innovation, and protect the rights of creators and consumers in the digital realm. New partnerships are forged between the public and private sectors, technology companies, and cultural organizations, creating a collaborative ecosystem where digital culture can thrive and flourish. And initiatives are launched to promote digital access and literacy, support digital content creators and entrepreneurs, and foster digital innovation and creativity in communities across the city.

And as the impact of these efforts begins to be felt, a new era of possibility and progress takes hold—a future where digital culture is not just a tool for economic growth, but a platform for social change, cultural expression, and human connection.

Cultural Diplomacy: Promoting Intercultural Dialogue Through Economic Exchange

In the midst of discussions surrounding cultural economics and creative industries, a notable subpoint emerges: cultural diplomacy—the strategic use of cultural exchange and economic cooperation to foster intercultural dialogue and understanding.

Dr. Olivia, Marcus, Sofia, and other influential figures reconvene, their minds brimming with the potential of cultural diplomacy to transcend borders and bridge divides.

Dr. Olivia, her scholarly expertise guiding her discourse, steps forward to address the assembly. "Cultural diplomacy represents a powerful tool for promoting peace, cooperation, and mutual understanding among nations," she begins. "By leveraging cultural exchange and economic collaboration, we can forge connections and build bridges that transcend political differences and promote shared values."

Marcus, drawing from his experiences as both an entrepreneur and a global citizen, adds his perspective to the conversation. "For too long, cultural diplomacy has been overshadowed by traditional forms of diplomacy," he asserts. "But today, we have the opportunity to harness the power of cultural exchange and economic cooperation to foster meaningful connections and build lasting relationships between peoples and nations."

Sofia, her passion for social justice intertwined with her advocacy for cultural exchange, emphasizes the importance of ensuring that cultural diplomacy is inclusive and equitable. "Cultural diplomacy has the potential to amplify voices that have long been marginalized or silenced," she declares. "But we must also ensure that it reflects the diversity of human experience and promotes the rights and dignity of all individuals and communities."

As the dialogue unfolds, a sense of hope and determination fills the room, as participants grapple with the complexities of promoting intercultural dialogue and understanding through economic exchange.

In the days and weeks that follow, Dr. Olivia, Marcus, Sofia, and their allies mobilize to advocate for a more inclusive and transformative approach to cultural diplomacy. They engage with policymakers, cultural institutions, and civil society organizations to develop strategies for promoting cultural exchange, supporting cultural entrepreneurship, and fostering economic cooperation across borders. They advocate for investments in cultural infrastructure, exchange programs, and initiatives that promote dialogue and understanding between diverse communities and cultures.

Together, they form a coalition for change, united in their commitment to harnessing the power of cultural diplomacy to build a more peaceful, prosperous, and interconnected world.

Their efforts begin to yield results, as policymakers embrace cultural diplomacy as a key pillar of foreign policy and international relations. New partnerships are forged between governments, cultural institutions, and private sector actors, creating a collaborative ecosystem where cultural exchange and economic cooperation can thrive. And initiatives are launched to promote cross-cultural dialogue, support cultural entrepreneurs and artists, and foster economic collaboration in areas such as tourism, trade, and investment.

And as the impact of these efforts begins to be felt, a new era of possibility and progress takes hold—a future where cultural diplomacy is not just a means of soft power, but a catalyst for positive change and global cooperation.

13

Chapter Thirteen: Happiness Economics and Well-Being

In a world fixated on economic growth and material wealth, a new chapter unfolds—one that delves into the essence of human flourishing and societal well-being. Dr. Olivia, Marcus, Sofia, and a host of influential figures gather once more, their hearts set on unraveling the mysteries of happiness economics and well-being.

Dr. Olivia, her scholarly prowess guiding her discourse, steps forth to address the assembly. "Happiness economics," she begins, "represents a paradigm shift in our understanding of prosperity. It transcends traditional measures of economic success, inviting us to explore the factors that truly contribute to human well-being—factors such as health, education, social connections, and a sense of purpose and belonging."

Marcus, his entrepreneurial spirit ignited by the prospect of a more fulfilling existence, adds his voice to the conversation. "For too long," he asserts, "we've equated happiness with material possessions and financial wealth. But today, we have the opportunity to redefine prosperity—to prioritize the

CHAPTER THIRTEEN: HAPPINESS ECONOMICS AND WELL-BEING

things that truly matter: meaningful relationships, personal growth, and a sense of community and belonging."

Sofia, her passion for social justice infusing her every word, underscores the importance of ensuring that well-being is accessible to all. "Happiness should not be a luxury reserved for the privileged few," she declares. "It should be a fundamental human right—a right that is accessible to people of all backgrounds, regardless of race, gender, or socioeconomic status."

As the dialogue unfolds, a sense of optimism and determination fills the room, as participants grapple with the complexities of measuring and promoting societal well-being.

In the days and weeks that follow, Dr. Olivia, Marcus, Sofia, and their allies mobilize to advocate for a more holistic approach to societal well-being. They engage with policymakers, researchers, and community leaders to develop strategies for promoting mental and physical health, fostering social connections, and creating environments that support human flourishing.

Together, they form a coalition for change, united in their commitment to building a society where happiness is not just a fleeting emotion, but a lasting state of being—a society where the pursuit of well-being takes precedence over the pursuit of wealth and material gain.

Their efforts begin to yield results, as policymakers embrace policies and initiatives that prioritize societal well-being. New partnerships are forged between government agencies, nonprofit organizations, and community groups, creating a collaborative ecosystem where happiness and fulfillment are seen as the true measures of success.

And as the impact of these efforts begins to be felt, a new

era of possibility and progress takes hold—a future where the pursuit of happiness is not just an individual endeavor, but a collective aspiration—a future where well-being is the ultimate currency, and where the true wealth of a nation lies in the health, happiness, and fulfillment of its people.

Beyond GDP: Alternative Measures of Progress and Well-Being

Within the exploration of happiness economics and well-being, a profound subpoint emerges: Beyond GDP—the quest for alternative measures of progress and societal well-being that transcend the confines of traditional economic indicators.

Dr. Olivia, Marcus, Sofia, and other influential figures reconvene, their minds ablaze with the possibility of redefining prosperity beyond mere material wealth.

Dr. Olivia, her scholarly acumen guiding her discourse, steps forth to address the assembly. "Beyond GDP," she begins, "is a call to action—a call to broaden our understanding of progress and prosperity. It challenges us to look beyond conventional economic metrics and consider the broader dimensions of human well-being, including health, education, environmental quality, and social cohesion."

Marcus, drawing from his experiences in entrepreneurship and societal impact, adds his voice to the conversation. "For too long," he asserts, "we've relied on GDP as the sole measure of success. But today, we have the opportunity to embrace a more holistic approach to progress—to recognize that true prosperity encompasses not only financial wealth, but also the health, happiness, and resilience of our communities."

Sofia, her passion for social justice fueling her advocacy, emphasizes the importance of ensuring that alternative measures of progress are inclusive and equitable. "Beyond GDP," she declares, "is about centering the voices of those who have been marginalized or excluded from traditional measures of prosperity. It's about valuing the contributions of all members of society, regardless of their socioeconomic status or background."

As the dialogue unfolds, a sense of urgency and possibility permeates the room, as participants grapple with the complexities of re-imagining progress in a rapidly changing world.

In the days and weeks that follow, Dr. Olivia, Marcus, Sofia, and their allies mobilize to advocate for the adoption of alternative measures of progress and well-being. They engage with policymakers, researchers, and civil society organizations to develop new metrics and indices that capture the multidimensional nature of prosperity.

Together, they form a coalition for change, united in their commitment to building a society where progress is measured not just by economic output, but by the health, happiness, and resilience of its people.

Their efforts begin to yield results, as policymakers embrace alternative measures of progress and well-being as valuable tools for guiding policy and decision-making. New partnerships are forged between governments, academia, and civil society, creating a collaborative ecosystem where diverse perspectives and experiences are valued and integrated into the fabric of society.

And as the impact of these efforts begins to be felt, a new era of possibility and progress takes hold—a future where prosperity is defined not by what we produce, but by how we live, love, and thrive together.

Subjective Well-Being: Understanding What Makes People Happy

As the exploration of happiness economics and well-being deepens, a profound subpoint emerges: Subjective Well-Being—the quest to understand the intricate factors that contribute to individual happiness and life satisfaction.

Dr. Olivia, Marcus, Sofia, and a cadre of influential figures reconvene, their minds brimming with curiosity about the subjective nature of human happiness.

Dr. Olivia, her scholarly insight guiding her discourse, steps forth to address the assembly. "Subjective Well-Being," she begins, "is a window into the human experience—a journey to uncover the elements that bring joy and fulfillment to our lives. It invites us to explore the interplay of personal circumstances, social connections, and inner states of being that shape our perception of happiness."

Marcus, drawing from his entrepreneurial ventures and personal introspection, adds his perspective to the conversation. "For too long," he asserts, "we've sought happiness in external achievements and possessions. But today, we have the opportunity to delve deeper—to recognize that true well-being comes from within, from nurturing our relationships, pursuing our passions, and finding meaning and purpose in our lives."

Sofia, her commitment to social justice imbuing her every word, emphasizes the importance of acknowledging the diversity of human experiences in the pursuit of well-being. "Subjective Well-Being," she declares, "is not a one-size-fits-all concept. It's about honoring the unique perspectives and realities of each individual, and creating environments that support their holistic flourishing."

As the dialogue unfolds, a sense of introspection and empathy permeates the room, as participants grapple with the intricacies of subjective well-being and its implications for societal progress.

In the days and weeks that follow, Dr. Olivia, Marcus, Sofia, and their allies embark on a journey of exploration and discovery, engaging with researchers, psychologists, and ordinary people from diverse backgrounds to unravel the mysteries of happiness.

Together, they form a coalition for understanding, united in their commitment to unraveling the complexities of human happiness and well-being.

Their efforts begin to yield insights, as they uncover the multifaceted nature of subjective well-being and the myriad factors that influence individual happiness.

And as the impact of their work reverberates, a new appreciation for the subjective nature of happiness takes hold—a recognition that true well-being cannot be measured by external metrics alone, but must also account for the rich tapestry of human emotions, experiences, and aspirations.

The Economics of Happiness: Determinants and Drivers

As the discussion on happiness economics and well-being unfolds, a compelling subpoint emerges: The Economics of Happiness—the exploration of the determinants and drivers that influence individual and societal levels of happiness.

Dr. Olivia, Marcus, Sofia, and a gathering of influential minds reconvene, their curiosity ignited by the prospect of uncovering the economic dimensions of human happiness.

Dr. Olivia, her scholarly expertise guiding her discourse, steps forth to address the assembly. "The Economics of Happiness," she begins, "is a journey into the underlying mechanisms that shape our subjective well-being. It invites us to examine the role of income, employment, social connections, and other economic factors in determining our levels of happiness."

Marcus, drawing from his entrepreneurial ventures and personal experiences, adds his voice to the conversation. "For too long," he asserts, "we've viewed happiness as an elusive pursuit, disconnected from the economic realities of our lives. But today, we have the opportunity to understand the ways in which economic factors can either enhance or detract from our well-being."

Sofia, her passion for social justice fueling her advocacy, emphasizes the importance of addressing economic inequalities in the pursuit of happiness. "The Economics of Happiness," she declares, "is also about recognizing the structural barriers that prevent certain groups from accessing opportunities for prosperity and fulfillment. It's about advocating for policies and initiatives that promote economic equity and social inclusion."

As the dialogue unfolds, a sense of urgency and determination fills the room, as participants grapple with the complexities of understanding the economic underpinnings of happiness.

In the days and weeks that follow, Dr. Olivia, Marcus, Sofia, and their allies embark on a quest to unravel the determinants and drivers of happiness. They engage with economists, psychologists, and policymakers to conduct research, analyze data, and develop strategies for promoting economic well-being and societal happiness.

Together, they form a coalition for change, united in their commitment to building an economy that prioritizes human flourishing over mere material wealth.

Their efforts begin to yield results, as policymakers embrace policies and initiatives that prioritize the well-being of citizens over narrow economic objectives. New partnerships are forged between government, business, and civil society, creating a collaborative ecosystem where economic prosperity and societal happiness go hand in hand.

And as the impact of their work reverberates, a new vision for the economy emerges—a vision where prosperity is measured not just by GDP growth, but by the happiness and well-being of all members of society.

Policy Implications of Happiness Research

As the discourse on happiness economics and well-being unfolds, a pivotal subpoint emerges: the Policy Implications of Happiness Research—the application of insights from the study of happiness to inform and shape public policy decisions.

Dr. Olivia, Marcus, Sofia, and a consortium of influential figures reconvene, their minds ablaze with the potential of translating happiness research into actionable policies for societal betterment.

Dr. Olivia, her scholarly acumen guiding her discourse, steps forth to address the assembly. "The Policy Implications of Happiness Research," she begins, "represent a transformative opportunity to align public policies with the fundamental goal of enhancing societal well-being. It invites us to rethink traditional approaches to governance and decision-making, placing human happiness and flourishing at the forefront of our priorities."

Marcus, drawing from his experiences in entrepreneurship and societal impact, adds his voice to the conversation. "For too long," he asserts, "we've relied on narrow metrics of success to guide policy decisions, often overlooking the holistic needs and aspirations of citizens. But today, we have the opportunity to embrace a more comprehensive approach—one that prioritizes the creation of policies and programs that promote happiness and well-being for all."

Sofia, her commitment to social justice fueling her advocacy, emphasizes the importance of addressing systemic inequalities in the pursuit of happiness-oriented policies. "The Policy Implications of Happiness Research," she declares, "must also reckon with the structural barriers that perpetuate injustice and inequity in our society. It's about centering the voices and experiences of marginalized communities and designing policies that ensure equitable access to opportunities for prosperity and fulfillment."

As the dialogue unfolds, a sense of purpose and determination permeates the room, as participants grapple with the complexities of translating happiness research into concrete policy recommendations.

In the days and weeks that follow, Dr. Olivia, Marcus, Sofia, and their allies mobilize to advocate for the integration of happiness-oriented policies into the fabric of governance. They engage with policymakers, legislators, and civil society organizations to raise awareness, build consensus, and drive meaningful change.

Together, they form a coalition for progress, united in their commitment to shaping a future where public policies are designed to maximize human happiness and well-being.

Their efforts begin to yield results, as governments embrace happiness research as a valuable tool for guiding decision-making and resource allocation. New initiatives are launched to promote mental health, foster social connections, and create environments that support human flourishing.

And as the impact of their work reverberates, a new paradigm of governance emerges—a paradigm where the success of policies is measured not just by economic growth, but by the happiness and well-being of citizens.

Workplace Well-Being: Creating Positive Organizational Cultures

Amidst the discourse on happiness economics and well-being, a crucial subpoint surfaces: Workplace Well-Being—the imperative of fostering positive organizational cultures that prioritize the happiness and flourishing of employees.

Dr. Olivia, Marcus, Sofia, and a cohort of influential minds reconvene, their focus shifting towards the pivotal role of workplaces in shaping individual happiness and societal well-being.

Dr. Olivia, her scholarly insight guiding her discourse, steps forth to address the assembly. "Workplace Well-Being," she begins, "is not merely a matter of productivity or profitability. It is a fundamental aspect of human flourishing—a space where individuals spend a significant portion of their lives and where their happiness and fulfillment can be profoundly influenced."

Marcus, drawing from his entrepreneurial ventures and personal experiences, adds his voice to the discussion. "For too long," he asserts, "we've viewed work as a means to an end, neglecting the impact it has on our overall well-being. But today, we have the opportunity to re-imagine workplaces as environments that nurture and support the holistic needs of employees—where purpose, belonging, and growth are central to organizational culture."

Sofia, her dedication to social justice infusing her advocacy, emphasizes the importance of addressing systemic inequalities and fostering inclusive workplaces. "Workplace Well-Being," she declares, "must also confront the structural barriers that perpetuate discrimination and inequity within organizations. It's about creating cultures of belonging and respect, where diversity is celebrated and every individual has the opportunity to thrive."

As the dialogue unfolds, a sense of urgency and determination permeates the room, as participants grapple with the complexities of transforming workplaces into spaces of well-being and fulfillment.

In the days and weeks that follow, Dr. Olivia, Marcus, Sofia, and their allies embark on a journey to advocate for positive organizational change. They engage with employers, human resource professionals, and workers' rights advocates to promote initiatives that prioritize employee well-being and foster positive workplace cultures.

Together, they form a coalition for progress, united in their commitment to creating workplaces where happiness and flourishing are not just aspirational goals, but tangible realities.

Their efforts begin to yield results, as organizations embrace initiatives such as flexible work arrangements, mental health support programs, and diversity and inclusion initiatives. New partnerships are forged between employers and employees, creating collaborative ecosystems where well-being is prioritized alongside productivity and performance.

And as the impact of their work reverberates, a new vision for workplaces emerges—a vision where employees are not just cogs in a machine, but valued members of a community where their happiness and fulfillment are central to organizational success.

Happiness and Public Policy: Toward a More Fulfilling Society

As the discourse on happiness economics and well-being progresses, a profound subpoint emerges: Happiness and Public Policy—the imperative of integrating happiness research into the fabric of governance to foster a more fulfilling and equitable society.

Dr. Olivia, Marcus, Sofia, and a consortium of influential figures reconvene, their minds ablaze with the potential of leveraging happiness insights to shape public policy for the betterment of all.

Dr. Olivia, her scholarly acumen guiding her discourse, steps forth to address the assembly. "Happiness and Public Policy," she begins, "represent a transformative opportunity to redefine the objectives of governance. It calls for a shift away from narrow economic metrics towards a more holistic understanding of societal well-being—one that prioritizes the happiness and flourishing of all citizens."

Marcus, drawing from his experiences in entrepreneurship and societal impact, adds his voice to the conversation. "For too long," he asserts, "we've measured the success of policies solely by their economic impact, overlooking their broader implications for human well-being. But today, we have the opportunity to adopt a more comprehensive approach—one that considers the social, environmental, and psychological dimensions of happiness in policy design and implementation."

Sofia, her commitment to social justice fueling her advocacy, emphasizes the importance of addressing systemic inequalities in the pursuit of happiness-oriented policies. "Happiness and Public Policy," she declares, "must also confront the structural barriers that perpetuate injustice and inequity in our society. It's about designing policies that promote equal opportunities, social inclusion, and environmental sustainability, creating conditions where every individual has the opportunity to lead a fulfilling life."

As the dialogue unfolds, a sense of purpose and determination permeates the room, as participants grapple with the complexities of integrating happiness research into public policy.

In the days and weeks that follow, Dr. Olivia, Marcus, Sofia, and their allies mobilize to advocate for a paradigm shift in governance. They engage with policymakers, legislators, and civil society organizations to promote the adoption of happiness-oriented policies at local, national, and international levels.

Together, they form a coalition for change, united in their commitment to shaping a future where public policies are designed to maximize human happiness and well-being.

Their efforts begin to yield results, as governments embrace happiness research as a valuable tool for guiding decision-making and resource allocation. New initiatives are launched to promote mental health, foster social connections, and create environments that support human flourishing.

And as the impact of their work reverberates, a new vision for governance emerges—a vision where the success of policies is measured not just by economic growth, but by the happiness and well-being of citizens.

Chapter Fourteen: Social Networks and Economic Behavior

In the bustling city of Lusaka, where Buildings loom tall and the hum of economic activity fills the air, a diverse group of individuals finds themselves entangled in the intricate web of social networks and economic behavior.

Dr. Olivia, Marcus, Sofia, and a cohort of influential figures gather once more, their minds alight with curiosity about the ways in which social connections shape economic decisions and outcomes.

Dr. Olivia, her scholarly wisdom guiding her discourse, steps forward to address the assembly. "Social Networks and Economic Behavior," she begins, "unveil the interconnectedness of human relationships and economic transactions. It invites us to explore how our social ties, whether familial, professional, or communal, influence our choices, preferences, and opportunities in the economic sphere."

Marcus, drawing from his entrepreneurial ventures and personal experiences, adds his voice to the conversation. "For too long," he asserts, "we've viewed economic decisions as solely rational and self-interested. But today, we have the opportunity to recognize the profound impact of social networks on our economic behavior. From word-of-mouth recommendations to collaborative ventures, our connections shape not only what we buy and sell but also how we innovate and create value."

Sofia, her commitment to social justice infusing her advocacy, emphasizes the importance of understanding how social networks can both empower and marginalize individuals in economic contexts. "Social Networks and Economic Behavior," she declares, "shed light on the mechanisms through which privilege and exclusion operate within our society. By examining the networks of power and influence that underpin economic transactions, we can work towards creating more inclusive and equitable systems that uplift all members of our community."

As the dialogue unfolds, a sense of camaraderie and exploration fills the room, as participants delve into the intricacies of social networks and their impact on economic behavior.

In the days and weeks that follow, Dr. Olivia, Marcus, Sofia, and their allies embark on a journey to unravel the dynamics of social networks in the economic realm. They engage with sociologists, economists, and community leaders to uncover the hidden connections and power structures that shape economic outcomes.

Together, they form a coalition for understanding, united in their quest to unravel the complexities of human interaction in the economic sphere.

Their efforts begin to yield insights, as they uncover the ways in which social networks facilitate information exchange, resource sharing, and collective action. New partnerships are forged, bridging divides and fostering collaboration across diverse communities.

And as the impact of their work reverberates, a new appreciation for the role of social networks in economic behavior emerges—a recognition that our connections with others not only shape our individual decisions but also have far-reaching implications for the broader economy.

Social Capital Theory: Networks and Norms in Economic Life

Within the vibrant cityscape of Lusaka, where the pulse of commerce beats in rhythm with the ebb and flow of social interaction, a new subpoint emerges: Social Capital Theory—exploring the intricate interplay between networks and norms in economic life.

Dr. Olivia, Marcus, Sofia, and their esteemed peers reconvene, their collective curiosity now honed on the fascinating realm of social capital and its profound impact on economic behavior.

Dr. Olivia, her scholarly acumen illuminating the discussion, steps forth to address the assembly. "Social Capital Theory," she begins, "unveils the rich tapestry of relationships and shared values that underpin economic activities. It delves into how the bonds of trust, reciprocity, and cooperation within social networks can serve as valuable resources for individuals and communities alike."

Marcus, drawing from his entrepreneurial experiences, adds his voice to the discourse. "Social Capital Theory," he asserts, "offers invaluable insights into the intangible assets that fuel economic success. Whether it's a network of mentors guiding

CHAPTER FOURTEEN: SOCIAL NETWORKS AND ECONOMIC BEHAVIOR

a budding entrepreneur or a tight-knit community supporting local businesses, the strength of our social connections often determines our ability to innovate, adapt, and thrive in the marketplace."

Sofia, her passion for social justice driving her advocacy, emphasizes the transformative potential of social capital in fostering inclusive economic development. "Social Capital Theory," she declares, "highlights the importance of nurturing connections that transcend traditional boundaries of class, race, and geography. By building bridges across diverse communities and empowering marginalized groups, we can unlock new opportunities for economic empowerment and shared prosperity."

As the dialogue unfolds, a palpable sense of resonance and inspiration fills the room, as participants delve deeper into the nuances of social capital and its implications for economic life.

In the days and weeks that follow, Dr. Olivia, Marcus, Sofia, and their allies embark on a journey to harness the power of social capital for positive change. They engage with community leaders, policymakers, and grassroots organizations to cultivate environments where trust, collaboration, and collective action can flourish.

Together, they form a coalition for social capital, united in their commitment to building stronger, more resilient communities where economic success is not just measured by individual wealth, but by the well-being and empowerment of all.

Their efforts begin to bear fruit, as social capital becomes recognized as a critical asset in economic development strategies. New initiatives are launched to foster social cohesion, civic engagement, and community resilience, laying the foundation for a more equitable and sustainable future.

And as the impact of their work reverberates, a new vision for economic life emerges—one where the bonds of social capital serve as the bedrock of prosperity, and where the values of trust, reciprocity, and cooperation shape the contours of a more just and inclusive society.

The Economics of Trust: Building Relationships in Economic Transactions

In the bustling metropolis of Lusaka, where the heartbeat of commerce echoes through its streets, a pivotal subpoint surfaces: The Economics of Trust—exploring the delicate dance of building relationships in economic transactions.

Dr. Olivia, Marcus, Sofia, and their esteemed colleagues reconvene, their attention now turned to the intricate dynamics of trust and its profound implications for economic behavior.

Dr. Olivia, her scholarly insight guiding her discourse, steps forward to address the gathering. "The Economics of Trust," she begins, "unveils the fundamental role that trust plays in facilitating economic exchange. It delves into how the presence or absence of trust can shape the decisions we make, the relationships we form, and the outcomes we achieve in the economic sphere."

Marcus, drawing from his entrepreneurial journey, adds his voice to the discussion. "Trust," he asserts, "is the currency of commerce—it underpins every transaction, negotiation, and partnership in the business world. From forging alliances with suppliers to winning the loyalty of customers, the ability to cultivate trust is essential for success in the marketplace."

CHAPTER FOURTEEN: SOCIAL NETWORKS AND ECONOMIC BEHAVIOR

Sofia, her dedication to social justice infusing her words, emphasizes the transformative power of trust in fostering collaboration and cooperation across diverse communities. "The Economics of Trust," she declares, "transcends mere transactions—it's about building bridges of understanding and empathy that span cultural, social, and economic divides. By nurturing trust, we can create environments where mutual respect and cooperation thrive, laying the foundation for sustainable economic growth and shared prosperity."

As the dialogue unfolds, a palpable sense of recognition and resonance fills the room, as participants grapple with the nuances of trust and its implications for economic interactions.

In the days and weeks that follow, Dr. Olivia, Marcus, Sofia, and their allies embark on a journey to cultivate trust in the economic landscape. They engage with business leaders, community organizers, and policymakers to promote transparency, integrity, and accountability in all facets of economic activity.

Together, they form a coalition for trust, united in their commitment to fostering environments where honesty, reliability, and fairness are valued as essential components of economic exchange.

Their efforts begin to yield results, as businesses adopt practices that prioritize ethical conduct and prioritize the long-term relationships over short-term gains. New partnerships are forged, built on a foundation of trust and mutual respect, creating ecosystems where innovation and collaboration flourish.

And as the impact of their work reverberates, a new paradigm for economic interactions emerges—one where trust is not just a commodity to be traded, but a cornerstone of resilient, thriving communities.

Network Effect: How Social Connections Shape Economic Outcomes

In the vibrant city of Lusaka, where the rhythm of economic activity harmonizes with the pulse of social interaction, a pivotal subpoint emerges: Network Effect—illuminating the profound impact of social connections on economic outcomes.

Dr. Olivia, Marcus, Sofia, and their esteemed colleagues reconvene, their focus now turned to the intricate dynamics of network effects and their far-reaching implications for economic behavior.

Dr. Olivia, her scholarly acumen guiding her discourse, steps forward to address the gathering. "The Network Effect," she begins, "reveals how the value of goods, services, and information can exponentially increase as they are shared and exchanged within social networks. It delves into how the structure and density of these networks shape the flow of resources, opportunities, and innovations in the economic landscape."

Marcus, drawing from his entrepreneurial endeavors, adds his voice to the dialogue. "Network effects," he asserts, "are the catalysts for growth and innovation—they amplify the impact of our actions and decisions, creating virtuous cycles of value creation and distribution. Whether it's the viral spread of a new product or the collaborative exchange of knowledge within a community, the power of networks to shape economic outcomes cannot be underestimated."

Sofia, her commitment to social justice driving her advocacy, emphasizes the transformative potential of network effects

CHAPTER FOURTEEN: SOCIAL NETWORKS AND ECONOMIC BEHAVIOR

in fostering inclusive economic development. "The Network Effect," she declares, "holds the key to unlocking opportunities for marginalized communities and underserved populations. By leveraging the collective resources and connections within social networks, we can empower individuals and businesses to overcome barriers and achieve sustainable growth and prosperity."

As the dialogue unfolds, a palpable sense of resonance and inspiration fills the room, as participants grapple with the complexities of network effects and their implications for economic progress.

In the days and weeks that follow, Dr. Olivia, Marcus, Sofia, and their allies embark on a journey to harness the power of network effects for positive change. They engage with entrepreneurs, policymakers, and community leaders to foster environments where networks can flourish and thrive.

Together, they form a coalition for network effects, united in their commitment to building stronger, more resilient communities where the benefits of economic growth are shared equitably among all members.

Their efforts begin to bear fruit, as networks become recognized as critical drivers of economic development and social progress. New initiatives are launched to promote collaboration, connectivity, and knowledge sharing, laying the foundation for a more inclusive and sustainable economy.

And as the impact of their work reverberates, a new vision for economic prosperity emerges—one where the power of networks is harnessed to create opportunities, foster innovation, and build a brighter future for all.

Social Influence and Customer Behavior

In the vibrant city of Lusaka, where the streets buzz with the energy of economic exchange, a pivotal subpoint emerges: Social Influence and Customer Behavior—shedding light on the powerful role of social connections in shaping consumer choices.

Dr. Olivia, Marcus, Sofia, and their esteemed colleagues reconvene, their focus now honed on understanding how social influence drives economic decisions.

Dr. Olivia, her scholarly insight guiding her discourse, steps forward to address the gathering. "Social Influence and Customer Behavior," she begins, "reveal the ways in which our interactions with others shape our preferences, perceptions, and purchasing decisions. It delves into the mechanisms through which social norms, peer pressure, and word-of-mouth recommendations influence consumer behavior in the marketplace."

Marcus, drawing from his experience as an entrepreneur, adds his perspective to the discussion. "Social influence," he asserts, "is a potent force in driving consumer behavior—it can turn a passing interest into a fervent desire, and a casual recommendation into a must-have purchase. By understanding the dynamics of social influence, businesses can harness the power of word-of-mouth marketing and social proof to cultivate loyal customer bases and drive sales."

Sofia, her commitment to social justice infusing her advocacy, emphasizes the importance of ethical considerations in leveraging social influence for positive change. "Social Influence and Customer Behavior," she declares, "challenge us to think critically about the ethical implications of marketing tactics that exploit social norms and peer pressure. By promoting transparency, authenticity, and respect for consumer autonomy, businesses can build trust and credibility with their audience, fostering long-term relationships built on mutual respect and shared values."

As the dialogue unfolds, a sense of urgency and introspection fills the room, as participants grapple with the ethical and practical dimensions of social influence in consumer behavior.

In the days and weeks that follow, Dr. Olivia, Marcus, Sofia, and their allies embark on a journey to navigate the complexities of social influence in the marketplace. They engage with psychologists, marketers, and consumer advocates to develop strategies that empower consumers to make informed choices while respecting their autonomy and agency.

Together, they form a coalition for ethical marketing, united in their commitment to promoting transparency, integrity, and social responsibility in all aspects of consumer engagement.

Their efforts begin to yield results, as businesses adopt practices that prioritize ethical marketing and consumer empowerment. New initiatives are launched to educate consumers about the impact of social influence and provide them with tools to make empowered decisions.

And as the impact of their work reverberates, a new paradigm for consumer behavior emerges—one where social influence is wielded responsibly and ethically, in service of promoting positive change and enhancing consumer well-being.

Online Social Networks: Implications for Marketing and Consumption

In the digital metropolis of Lusaka, where virtual connections weave a web of influence, a pivotal subpoint emerges: Online Social Networks—exploring their profound implications for marketing and consumption.

Dr. Olivia, Marcus, Sofia, and their esteemed colleagues reconvene, their attention now turned to the dynamic world of online social networks and its impact on economic behavior.

Dr. Olivia, her scholarly insight guiding her discourse, steps forward to address the gathering. "Online Social Networks," she begins, "have transformed the landscape of marketing and consumption, reshaping how businesses engage with customers and how individuals make purchasing decisions. It delves into the ways in which social media platforms, influencer marketing, and online communities influence consumer behavior in the digital age."

Marcus, drawing from his entrepreneurial ventures, adds his perspective to the discussion. "Online social networks," he asserts, "have democratized the marketplace, giving voice to consumers and providing businesses with unprecedented opportunities to connect with their target audience. From viral marketing campaigns to personalized recommendations, the power of online networks to drive consumer engagement and loyalty cannot be overstated."

Sofia, her commitment to social justice guiding her advocacy, emphasizes the importance of ethical considerations in online marketing practices. "Online Social Networks," she declares, "pose unique challenges and opportunities for businesses seeking to navigate the digital landscape. By prioritizing authenticity, transparency, and respect for consumer privacy, businesses can build trust and credibility with their online audience, fostering meaningful connections that transcend the digital realm."

As the dialogue unfolds, a sense of excitement and uncertainty fills the room, as participants grapple with the complexities of online social networks and their implications for economic behavior.

In the days and weeks that follow, Dr. Olivia, Marcus, Sofia, and their allies embark on a journey to harness the power of online social networks for positive change. They engage with digital marketers, social media influencers, and tech innovators to develop strategies that prioritize ethical engagement and consumer empowerment in the online sphere.

Together, they form a coalition for digital ethics, united in their commitment to promoting responsible practices and fostering a digital environment that prioritizes user well-being and privacy.

Their efforts begin to bear fruit, as businesses adopt strategies that prioritize authenticity and transparency in their online interactions. New initiatives are launched to educate consumers about their digital rights and empower them to make informed choices in the online marketplace.

And as the impact of their work reverberates, a new era of online engagement emerges—one where businesses and consumers coexist in a digital ecosystem built on trust, integrity, and respect.

Policy Approaches to Nurturing Social Capital

In the heart of Lusaka, where the pulse of society beats in rhythm with economic exchanges, a critical subpoint emerges: Policy Approaches to Nurturing Social Capital—exploring the role of governance in fostering vibrant social networks for economic prosperity.

Dr. Olivia, Marcus, Sofia, and their esteemed colleagues reconvene, their focus now turned to understanding how policy interventions can cultivate and nurture social capital for the benefit of all.

Dr. Olivia, her scholarly wisdom guiding her discourse, steps forward to address the assembly. "Policy Approaches to Nurturing Social Capital," she begins, "illuminate the ways in which government policies and programs can shape the formation and strength of social networks. It delves into strategies for promoting community engagement, trust-building, and social cohesion to enhance economic resilience and well-being."

Marcus, drawing from his entrepreneurial experiences, adds his voice to the discussion. "Social capital," he asserts, "is the bedrock of thriving economies—it fosters collaboration, innovation, and resilience in the face of challenges. By investing in policies that strengthen social ties and promote civic engagement, governments can create environments where businesses can flourish and individuals can thrive."

Sofia, her dedication to social justice fueling her advocacy, emphasizes the importance of inclusive policies that address systemic inequalities and empower marginalized communities. "Policy Approaches to Nurturing Social Capital," she declares, "must prioritize equity, diversity, and inclusion to ensure that all members of society have access to the resources and opportunities needed to participate fully in economic life."

As the dialogue unfolds, a sense of urgency and determination fills the room, as participants grapple with the complexities of social policy and its implications for economic development.

In the days and weeks that follow, Dr. Olivia, Marcus, Sofia, and their allies embark on a journey to advocate for policies that prioritize social capital as a key driver of economic prosperity. They engage with policymakers, community leaders, and grassroots organizations to develop strategies that promote social cohesion, civic participation, and collective action.

Together, they form a coalition for social policy reform, united in their commitment to building inclusive, resilient communities where the benefits of economic growth are shared equitably among all members.

Their efforts begin to yield results, as governments adopt policies that prioritize investments in social infrastructure, community development, and support for grassroots initiatives. New programs are launched to foster cross-sectoral collaboration and empower communities to address local challenges and opportunities.

And as the impact of their work reverberates, a new vision for social policy emerges—one where governments play a proactive role in nurturing social capital as a foundation for sustainable economic development and human flourishing.

15

Chapter Fifteen: Human Rights and Economic Development

In the bustling city of Lusaka, where the aspirations of humanity converge with the dynamics of economic progress, a pivotal chapter unfolds: Human Rights and Economic Development—a narrative that intertwines the quest for prosperity with the pursuit of justice and dignity for all.

Dr. Olivia, Marcus, Sofia, and their esteemed colleagues gather once more, their minds focused on the intersection of human rights and economic advancement.

Dr. Olivia, her scholarly insight guiding her discourse, steps forward to address the assembly. "Human Rights and Economic Development," she begins, "explore the intrinsic link between human rights principles and sustainable economic growth. It delves into how upholding fundamental rights—such as the right to education, health, and decent work—lays the groundwork for inclusive prosperity and social progress."

Marcus, drawing from his entrepreneurial journey, adds his perspective to the discussion. "Human rights," he asserts, "are not only moral imperatives but also economic imperatives—they create the conditions for individuals to fully participate in and contribute to the economy. By ensuring equal opportunities and protections for all, we lay the foundation for a more resilient and dynamic economy."

Sofia, her commitment to social justice driving her advocacy, emphasizes the importance of centering human rights in economic policy and practice. "Human Rights and Economic Development," she declares, "challenge us to confront systemic inequalities and injustices that hinder human potential and economic progress. By prioritizing human dignity, equity, and social inclusion, we can build economies that serve the needs and aspirations of all people."

As the dialogue unfolds, a sense of purpose and resolve fills the room, as participants grapple with the complexities of aligning economic goals with human rights principles.

In the days and weeks that follow, Dr. Olivia, Marcus, Sofia, and their allies embark on a journey to advocate for policies and practices that uphold human rights as integral to economic development. They engage with policymakers, business leaders, and civil society organizations to promote inclusive and rights-based approaches to economic governance.

Together, they form a coalition for human rights and economic justice, united in their commitment to building societies where economic progress is inseparable from human flourishing and dignity.

Their efforts begin to yield results, as governments adopt policies that prioritize human rights in economic decision-making, businesses embrace responsible practices that respect labor rights and environmental sustainability, and communities mobilize to demand accountability and transparency in economic systems.

And as the impact of their work reverberates, a new vision for economic development emerges—one where human rights are not only respected but also celebrated as the cornerstone of prosperity and well-being for all.

Economic Rights: The Foundation of Human Dignity

As the discourse on Human Rights and Economic Development unfolds, a critical subpoint emerges: Economic Rights—The Foundation of Human Dignity—a narrative that illuminates the intrinsic link between economic rights and the preservation of human dignity.

Dr. Olivia, Marcus, Sofia, and their esteemed colleagues gather once more, their attention now turned to the fundamental rights that underpin economic well-being and dignity for all.

Dr. Olivia, her scholarly insight guiding her discourse, steps forward to address the assembly. "Economic Rights," she begins, "serve as the bedrock of human dignity—they encompass the right to work, to fair wages, to social security, and to an adequate standard of living. These rights are not mere luxuries but essential elements for individuals to lead fulfilling and dignified lives."

Marcus, drawing from his entrepreneurial experiences, adds his perspective to the discussion. "Economic rights," he asserts, "empower individuals to participate meaningfully in economic life—they provide the foundation for entrepreneurship, innovation, and economic self-sufficiency. By guaranteeing economic rights, we uphold the dignity of every person and foster a society where everyone has the opportunity to thrive."

CHAPTER FIFTEEN: HUMAN RIGHTS AND ECONOMIC DEVELOPMENT

Sofia, her dedication to social justice fueling her advocacy, emphasizes the importance of collective action in safeguarding economic rights for all. "Economic Rights," she declares, "are not granted—they are claimed through collective struggle and solidarity. It is our responsibility to advocate for policies and practices that ensure the realization of economic rights for every individual, particularly those who are marginalized or disadvantaged."

As the dialogue unfolds, a sense of urgency and determination fills the room, as participants grapple with the implications of economic rights for human dignity and social justice.

In the days and weeks that follow, Dr. Olivia, Marcus, Sofia, and their allies embark on a journey to champion economic rights as non-negotiable principles of human dignity. They engage with policymakers, labor unions, and grassroots organizations to advocate for policies that guarantee fair wages, protect workers' rights, and provide social safety nets for those in need.

Together, they form a coalition for economic justice, united in their commitment to building economies that prioritize the well-being and dignity of all people.

Their efforts begin to yield results, as governments enact legislation to protect economic rights, businesses adopt fair labor practices, and communities mobilize to demand economic justice for all.

And as the impact of their work reverberates, a new paradigm for economic development emerges—one where economic rights are recognized as essential components of human dignity and social progress.

The Role of International Human Rights Law in Economic Development

As the discourse on Human Rights and Economic Development unfolds, a crucial subpoint emerges: The Role of International Human Rights Law in Economic Development—a narrative that explores the intersection of legal frameworks and economic progress in the global arena.

Dr. Olivia, Marcus, Sofia, and their esteemed colleagues reconvene, their focus now turned to the influence of international human rights law on shaping economic development policies and practices.

Dr. Olivia, her scholarly insight guiding her discourse, steps forward to address the assembly. "International Human Rights Law," she begins, "provides a framework for promoting economic development that is grounded in principles of justice, equality, and dignity. It establishes standards and obligations that governments and businesses must uphold to ensure that economic progress benefits all members of society."

Marcus, drawing from his experiences navigating global markets, adds his perspective to the discussion. "International human rights law," he asserts, "provides a level playing field for economic actors by setting clear expectations and accountability mechanisms. By adhering to international human rights standards, governments and businesses can build trust, foster cooperation, and attract investment in a globalized world."

Sofia, her dedication to human rights advocacy fueling her passion, emphasizes the importance of international solidarity in advancing economic justice. "International Human Rights Law," she declares, "serves as a powerful tool for amplifying the voices of marginalized communities and holding powerful actors accountable for their actions. By leveraging international mechanisms and partnerships, we can address global challenges such as poverty, inequality, and environmental degradation in a collaborative and coordinated manner."

As the dialogue unfolds, a sense of determination and solidarity permeates the room, as participants grapple with the complexities of international human rights law and its implications for economic development.

In the days and weeks that follow, Dr. Olivia, Marcus, Sofia, and their allies embark on a journey to promote the integration of human rights principles into international economic policies and agreements. They engage with diplomats, policymakers, and civil society organizations to advocate for the adoption of rights-based approaches to trade, investment, and development cooperation.

Together, they form a coalition for human rights and economic justice on the global stage, united in their commitment to building a more equitable and sustainable world for future generations.

Their efforts begin to yield results, as international institutions and governments incorporate human rights considerations into their economic decision-making processes. New partnerships are forged to address transnational challenges and promote inclusive economic growth that leaves no one behind.

And as the impact of their work reverberates across borders, a new paradigm for international economic relations emerges—one where human rights are recognized as essential drivers of development and prosperity.

Economic Justice and Human Rights Advocacy

As the discussion on Human Rights and Economic Development progresses, a crucial subpoint emerges: Economic Justice and Human Rights Advocacy—a narrative that underscores the vital role of advocacy in advancing economic rights and social justice for all.

Dr. Olivia, Marcus, Sofia, and their esteemed colleagues reconvene, their focus now directed towards the power of advocacy in promoting economic justice within the framework of human rights.

Dr. Olivia, her scholarly wisdom guiding her discourse, steps forward to address the assembly. "Economic Justice and Human Rights Advocacy," she begins, "highlight the indispensable role of grassroots movements, civil society organizations, and individual activists in holding governments and corporations accountable for upholding economic rights. Through advocacy efforts, marginalized communities can amplify their voices, mobilize for change, and demand accountability from those in power."

Marcus, drawing from his experiences as a change-maker, adds his voice to the discussion. "Economic justice," he asserts, "is not bestowed—it is fought for. Through strategic advocacy campaigns, we can raise awareness about economic inequalities, mobilize public support for policy reforms, and challenge unjust economic structures that perpetuate poverty and exclusion. By uniting in solidarity, we can drive meaningful change and create a more equitable and inclusive society for all."

Sofia, her commitment to social justice unwavering, emphasizes the importance of collective action in advancing human rights advocacy. "Economic Justice and Human Rights Advocacy," she declares, "are interconnected struggles that require solidarity across borders and sectors. By building alliances, sharing resources, and amplifying diverse voices, we can build a powerful movement for economic justice that leaves no one behind."

As the dialogue unfolds, a sense of urgency and determination fills the room, as participants recognize the transformative potential of advocacy in shaping economic policies and practices.

In the days and weeks that follow, Dr. Olivia, Marcus, Sofia, and their allies embark on a journey to harness the power of advocacy to advance economic justice and human rights. They organize rallies, conduct research, and engage with policymakers to push for reforms that prioritize the needs of the most vulnerable and marginalized members of society.

Together, they form a coalition of advocates for economic justice, united in their commitment to building a world where economic rights are respected, protected, and fulfilled for all.

Their efforts begin to yield results, as governments enact policies that address economic inequalities, businesses adopt fair labor practices, and communities mobilize for change.

And as the impact of their advocacy reverberates, a new narrative of hope and possibility emerges—one where economic justice is not just a distant dream, but a tangible reality for all people.

Gender Equality as a Human Right: Promoting Women's Empowerment

As the discourse on Human Rights and Economic Development continues, a pivotal subpoint emerges: Gender Equality as a Human Right: Promoting Women's Empowerment—a narrative that sheds light on the imperative of advancing gender equality as a cornerstone of human rights and economic progress.

Dr. Olivia, Marcus, Sofia, and their esteemed colleagues reconvene, their attention now focused on the critical role of promoting women's empowerment within the framework of human rights.

Dr. Olivia, her scholarly insight guiding her discourse, steps forward to address the assembly. "Gender Equality as a Human Right," she begins, "is not only a moral imperative but also an economic imperative. By ensuring equal rights and opportunities for women, we unlock their full potential as agents of change, innovation, and economic growth. Gender equality is not just about fairness—it's about maximizing human capital and building inclusive economies that benefit everyone."

Marcus, drawing from his experiences in the business world, adds his perspective to the discussion. "Promoting women's empowerment," he asserts, "is not only the right thing to do—it's also smart economics. Studies show that companies with diverse leadership teams perform better financially. By breaking down barriers to women's participation in the economy, we can unleash a wave of innovation, productivity, and prosperity that benefits society as a whole."

Sofia, her dedication to social justice unwavering, emphasizes the importance of intersectional approaches to gender equality. "Gender Equality as a Human Right," she declares, "must address the intersecting forms of discrimination that women face based on race, class, sexuality, and other factors. True gender equality requires dismantling systems of oppression and building inclusive societies where all women can thrive, regardless of their background or identity."

As the dialogue unfolds, a sense of urgency and solidarity fills the room, as participants recognize the transformative potential of promoting women's empowerment for advancing human rights and economic development.

In the days and weeks that follow, Dr. Olivia, Marcus, Sofia, and their allies embark on a journey to advocate for policies and practices that promote gender equality and women's empowerment. They engage with policymakers, business leaders, and community organizations to push for reforms that address gender-based discrimination, promote women's leadership, and ensure equal opportunities for all.

Together, they form a coalition for gender equality, united in their commitment to building a world where women's rights are respected, protected, and fulfilled in every sphere of life.

Their efforts begin to yield results, as governments adopt gender-responsive policies, businesses implement gender-inclusive practices, and communities mobilize for change.

And as the impact of their work reverberates, a new narrative of empowerment and equality emerges—one where women's rights are upheld as fundamental human rights, and every woman has the opportunity to realize her full potential and contribute to a more just, equitable, and prosperous world.

Indigenous Rights and Economic Development

As the dialogue on Human Rights and Economic Development evolves, a significant subpoint emerges: Indigenous Rights and Economic Development—a narrative that underscores the importance of recognizing and upholding the rights of indigenous peoples as essential for sustainable economic progress.

Dr. Olivia, Marcus, Sofia, and their esteemed colleagues reconvene, their focus now turned towards the critical intersection of indigenous rights and economic development.

Dr. Olivia, her scholarly insight guiding her discourse, steps forward to address the assembly. "Indigenous Rights and Economic Development," she begins, "represent a vital aspect of human rights that must be safeguarded and respected. Indigenous peoples have unique cultural, spiritual, and economic connections to their lands, which are often threatened by unsustainable development projects and resource extraction. By recognizing and protecting indigenous rights, we can promote inclusive economic growth that respects the dignity, autonomy, and self-determination of indigenous communities."

Marcus, drawing from his experiences advocating for corporate responsibility, adds his perspective to the discussion. "Indigenous rights," he asserts, "are not just moral imperatives—they are also economic imperatives. Companies that engage in meaningful consultation and partnership with indigenous communities are more likely to achieve long-term success and avoid costly conflicts and reputational damage. By embracing indigenous rights, businesses can foster mutually beneficial relationships that promote sustainable development and shared prosperity."

Sofia, her commitment to social justice unwavering, emphasizes the importance of centering indigenous voices in economic decision-making processes. "Indigenous Rights and Economic Development," she declares, "require genuine partnership and collaboration between indigenous peoples, governments, and other stakeholders. By respecting indigenous knowledge, traditions, and governance systems, we can harness the wisdom of indigenous communities to address pressing environmental and social challenges and build a more resilient and equitable future for all."

As the dialogue unfolds, a sense of reverence and solidarity permeates the room, as participants recognize the profound significance of upholding indigenous rights in the pursuit of economic development.

In the days and weeks that follow, Dr. Olivia, Marcus, Sofia, and their allies embark on a journey to advocate for policies and practices that respect and protect indigenous rights. They engage with governments, corporations, and international organizations to promote indigenous-led development initiatives, strengthen land rights, and foster inclusive economic opportunities for indigenous communities.

Together, they form a coalition for indigenous rights and economic justice, united in their commitment to building a world where indigenous peoples' rights are upheld, their voices are heard, and their contributions are valued and respected.

Their efforts begin to yield results, as governments adopt policies that recognize and protect indigenous rights, companies engage in meaningful consultation and partnership with indigenous communities, and indigenous-led enterprises thrive.

And as the impact of their work reverberates, a new narrative of empowerment and solidarity emerges—one where indigenous peoples' rights are upheld as fundamental human rights, and economic development is pursued in harmony with the values and aspirations of indigenous communities.

Human Rights-Based Approaches to Economic Policy Making

As the conversation on Human Rights and Economic Development unfolds, another crucial subpoint emerges: Human Rights-Based Approaches to Economic Policy Making—a narrative that underscores the imperative of integrating human rights principles into economic policy to ensure equitable and sustainable development.

Dr. Olivia, Marcus, Sofia, and their esteemed colleagues reconvene, their attention now directed towards the essential role of human rights-based approaches in shaping economic policy.

Dr. Olivia, her scholarly insight guiding her discourse, steps forward to address the assembly. "Human Rights-Based Approaches to Economic Policy Making," she begins, "offer a transformative framework for advancing social justice, dignity, and equality within our economic systems. By centering human rights principles such as non-discrimination, participation, transparency, and accountability, we can ensure that economic policies are designed and implemented in ways that prioritize the well-being and rights of all individuals, particularly the most marginalized and vulnerable."

Marcus, drawing from his experiences in business and advocacy, adds his perspective to the discussion. "Human rights," he asserts, "must be at the forefront of economic decision-making processes. By adopting human rights-based approaches, governments can design policies that address systemic inequalities, promote inclusive growth, and empower individuals to exercise their economic rights. Businesses, too, have a responsibility to respect human rights throughout their operations, from supply chains to employment practices, and to contribute positively to the realization of human rights within their spheres of influence."

Sofia, her dedication to social justice unwavering, emphasizes the importance of participatory approaches in economic policy making. "Human Rights-Based Approaches to Economic Policy Making," she declares, "require meaningful engagement with affected communities and stakeholders. By involving people in the decision-making process, governments can ensure that policies reflect the diverse needs and priorities of the population and are responsive to their lived realities. Participation fosters ownership, accountability, and legitimacy, laying the groundwork for policies that truly serve the interests of all."

As the dialogue unfolds, a sense of urgency and determination fills the room, as participants recognize the transformative potential of human rights-based approaches in shaping economic policy for the benefit of all.

In the days and weeks that follow, Dr. Olivia, Marcus, Sofia, and their allies embark on a journey to advocate for the adoption of human rights-based approaches in economic policy making at all levels of governance. They engage with policymakers, civil society organizations, and international institutions to promote the integration of human rights principles into economic policy frameworks, legislation, and decision-making processes.

Together, they form a coalition for human rights and economic justice, united in their commitment to building a world where economic policies are guided by principles of human dignity, equality, and social justice.

Their efforts begin to yield results, as governments adopt human rights-based approaches in the design and implementation of economic policies, businesses align their practices with human rights standards, and communities are empowered to advocate for their economic rights.

And as the impact of their work reverberates, a new narrative of hope and possibility emerges—one where economic policies are instruments of justice and empowerment, and where human rights are upheld as the foundation of a fair, inclusive, and sustainable economy for all.

CHAPTER FIFTEEN: HUMAN RIGHTS AND ECONOMIC DEVELOPMENT

Synopsis:

In the bustling city of Lusaka, where Buildings tower over crowded streets and the relentless pursuit of profit fuels every transaction, a diverse cast of characters finds themselves entangled in the complexities of economic theory and practice. At the heart of their journey lies the enigmatic book "Humanomics: Integrating Humanity into Economic Theory and Practice," which promises to revolutionize their understanding of economics and reshape their worldviews.

Characters:

1. Dr. Olivia: A brilliant economist disillusioned by the cold calculations of traditional economic models. Dr. Olivia embarks on a quest to unravel the mysteries of humanomics and challenge the status quo.

2. Marcus: A young entrepreneur whose relentless pursuit of success has left him feeling empty and disconnected from the world around him. Marcus stumbles upon "Humanomics" and becomes determined to reconcile profit with human values.

3. Sofia : An idealistic activist fighting against economic inequality and social injustice in Lusaka's marginalized communities. Sofia sees "Humanomics" as a beacon of hope for creating a more equitable society.

4. Professor Samuel: A wise mentor and former colleague of Dr. Olivia, Professor Samuel possesses a deep understanding of human behavior and its implications for economic systems. He serves as a guide for those seeking enlightenment through humanomics.

5. Rajesh Patel: A struggling small business owner caught in the crossfire of corporate greed and economic uncertainty.

Rajesh's journey with "Humanomics" leads him to discover the power of community and cooperation in overcoming adversity.

Plot:

As Dr. Olivia delves into the pages of "Humanomics," she begins to question the fundamental assumptions of mainstream economics. With each revelation, she finds herself drawn deeper into a world where human values and empathy reign supreme over profit margins.

Meanwhile, Marcus's latest business venture teeters on the brink of collapse as ethical dilemmas threaten to undermine his success. Desperate for guidance, he turns to "Humanomics" in search of a solution that balances financial prosperity with social responsibility.

Sofia's grassroots activism brings her face-to-face with the harsh realities of economic inequality, inspiring her to seek out alternative approaches to addressing social injustice. Through "Humanomics," she discovers the transformative potential of community-led initiatives and solidarity economies.

As the paths of Dr. Olivia, Marcus, Sofia, and Rajesh converge, they find themselves embroiled in a battle for the soul of Lusaka. Against the backdrop of corporate greed and political corruption, they must harness the principles of humanomics to forge a new vision for economic prosperity—one that prioritizes the well-being of all citizens over the pursuit of wealth.

In the end, their journey culminates in a groundbreaking conference where they present their findings to an international audience of economists, policymakers, and activists. Together, they chart a course toward a future where humanity and economics are no longer at odds, but inextricably intertwined in a harmonious dance of progress and prosperity."

About the Author

Goodson Mumba is a multifaceted individual known for his diverse expertise and prolific contributions across various fields. As an infopreneur, thought leader, and spiritual leader, he has inspired countless individuals through his insightful teachings and impactful writings. Mumba is also an accomplished author, with several notable works to his name, including "Understanding Corporate Worship," "The Years I Spent in a Week," "Management By Harmony," "The CEO's Diary," "Change to Change" and "Creative Thinking for results" His literary works span topics ranging from business management to personal development and spirituality, reflecting his broad range of interests and insights.

With a Master of Business Leadership (MBL) and a Bachelor of Arts in Theology (BTh), Mumba brings a unique blend of business acumen and spiritual wisdom to his work. His educational background is further enriched by a Group Diploma in Management Studies, providing him with a solid foundation in organizational dynamics and leadership principles. Additionally, Mumba holds diplomas in Education Psychology,

Leadership and Management Styles, Organizational Behavior, Financial Accounting, Economic Growth and Development, and Project Management, showcasing his commitment to continuous learning and professional development.

Mumba's expertise extends beyond traditional academic disciplines, encompassing areas such as Neuro-Linguistic Programming (NLP) and Positive Psychology. His diverse skill set is complemented by a range of certifications, including Creative Problem Solving and Decision Making, Life Coaching Fundamentals and Techniques, Professional Life Coaching, and Performance Management System Design. These certifications reflect Mumba's dedication to equipping himself with the tools and knowledge necessary to empower others and drive positive change.

As an author, Mumba's writings reflect his deep understanding of human nature, organizational dynamics, and spiritual principles. His works offer practical insights, actionable strategies, and inspirational guidance for individuals seeking personal growth, professional success, and spiritual fulfillment. Mumba's holistic approach to life and leadership resonates with readers worldwide, making him a respected figure in both the business and spiritual communities.

Overall, Goodson Mumba's diverse background, extensive knowledge, and profound insights make him a sought-after speaker, mentor, and author. His commitment to excellence, lifelong learning, and service to others continues to inspire individuals to unlock their full potential and lead lives of purpose and significance.

Goodson Mumba is renowned for initiating the concept of Management by Harmony, revolutionizing traditional management practices with a focus on balanced and holistic approaches. He has authored two influential books on this subject: "Introduction to Management by Harmony" and its sequel, "Management by Harmony."

Mumba's work has significantly impacted the field, offering innovative strategies for fostering organizational harmony and efficiency. His contributions continue to shape contemporary management theories and practices.

www.ingramcontent.com/pod-product-compliance
Lightning Source LLC
Chambersburg PA
CBHW071827210526
45479CB00001B/24